Minding the Helm

An Unlikely Career in the U.S. Coast Guard

Kevin P. Gilheany

Louise,

All the best!

Number 14 in the North Texas Military Biography and Memoir Series
University of North Texas Press
Denton, Texas

10 9 8 7 6 5 4 3 2 1

Permissions:
University of North Texas Press
1155 Union Circle #311336
Denton, TX 76203-5017

The paper used in this book meets the minimum requirements of the American
National Standard for Permanence of Paper for Printed Library Materials,
z39.48.1984. Binding materials have been chosen for durability.

Library of Congress Cataloging-in-Publication Data

Names: Gilheany, Kevin P., 1963- author.
Title: Minding the helm : an unlikely career in the U.S. Coast Guard / Kevin P. Gilheany.
Other titles: North Texas military biography and memoir series ; no. 14.
Description: Denton, Texas : University of North Texas Press, [2019] |
Series: Number 14 in the North Texas military biography and memoir
series | Includes bibliographical references and index.
Identifiers: LCCN 2019002205| ISBN 9781574417500 (cloth
: alk. paper) | ISBN 9781574417562 (e-book)
Subjects: LCSH: Gilheany, Kevin P., 1963- | United States. Coast Guard--Officers--
Biography. | Bagpipers--Biography. | Band musicians--Biography. | U.S. Coast
Guard Pipe Band. | United States. Coast Guard--History--20th century.
Classification: LCC V63.G47 A3 2019 | DDC 363.28/6092 [B] --dc23
LC record available at https://lccn.loc.gov/2019002205

Minding the Helm:An Unlikely Career in the U.S. Coast Guard is Number 14
in the North Texas Military Biography and Memoir Series

The electronic edition of this book was made possible by
the support of the Vick Family Foundation.

Jacket and page design by Joseph Parenteau

For Stefanie and Emma,

and all the men and women of the

United States Coast Guard.

Contents

Preface

This is a work of creative nonfiction. The events portrayed have been described to the best of my recollection. While all of the stories in this book are true, some of the names and identifying details have been changed to protect the privacy of the people involved.

Though I often claim a photographic memory when arguing with my wife about "what was said" between us, I will not make such a claim with regard to the conversations in this book. In all cases, the dialogue has been recreated to the best of my recollection. While these conversations are not literal transcriptions, they have been retold as accurately as my memory will allow. In all instances the essence of the dialogue is accurate.

Acknowledgements

Writing this memoir has been a long and rewarding process, one that I could not have finished if not for the loving support and excellent copy-editing skills of my wife Stefanie, who put up with my endless revisions, typos, and spelling errors. I must also thank Emma, the best daughter anyone could be blessed with, for allowing me the time to complete this project without ever once complaining or making me feel guilty.

The project would not have begun if not for the Loyola University New Orleans Walker Percy Institute, which kicked off this process with a Creative Nonfiction Course that gave me the confidence and feedback necessary to continue. I especially want to thank some special students in that class, including Virginia Campbell, Karen Eberle, Meredith Cunningham, Christine Miller, and Maria Motch, who had the foresight to continue our writing by forming a writers' group. The structure of deadlines and the excellent feedback from the group served as a much needed motivating force.

I would like to thank my beta readers, Dr. Chris Wiseman and Lola Dart, for their generosity and objective input, which was extremely valuable to me in understanding the differing perspectives of readers, and my friends Jo Huey and Ed Moise, for reading the final draft and providing their support and encouragement.

Ron Chrisman, and the editorial board at the University of North Texas Press, deserve special thanks for taking a chance on this first-time author, as well as their peer reviewers, Dr. C. Douglas Kroll and Professor Jim Dolbow, whose positive reviews and great insight helped to make this book a reality.

Introduction

Growing up in Manhattan, I didn't realize we were poor. I was a happy kid. Although we never ventured more than a few hours from my place of birth on the edge of Central Park, I was exposed to many things, including the South Street Seaport, the Staten Island Ferry, and the Coast Guard Academy's sailing ship *Eagle*. My mother was just trying to keep us busy and out of trouble. She didn't know that she was inspiring lifelong dreams in a little boy. My mother believed in the power of dreaming good dreams, but I don't think she ever thought there was much chance of them becoming reality. For her, the dream was enough. I didn't know if dreams could come true either, but I decided to find out.

There is no better work than that which is aligned with our core principles. Working in the U.S. Coast Guard was exactly that for me. As a kid, I was drawn to its humanitarian mission, as well as the romance and excitement of going to sea. I enlisted in the Coast Guard at the age of nineteen even though I was an unlikely recruit: I didn't know how to swim, I was out of shape, and I liked to drink a bit too much. Still, I went off to boot camp on January 24, 1983.

Passing the swim test in boot camp is still one of the biggest accomplishments of my life. It was blind faith in God, and in myself, along with sheer determination to not return home as a failure that got me through it. I was extremely grateful for having been able to join the ranks of the U.S. Coast Guard. As a result, I wanted to do excellent work in whatever task I was assigned, including cleaning toilets. As I continued to do excellent work, doors continued to open for me.

I was assigned to a number of ships and had many an adventure at sea including experiencing thirty-foot seas, surviving freak waves, capturing drug smugglers, rescuing Haitian migrants, recovering Space Shuttle *Challenger* debris, and serving as helmsman on the tall ship *Eagle* as she passed the Statue of Liberty during Operation Sail 1986. It was everything I ever imagined and more, and it provided me with enough sea stories to fill a book. Following sea duty, I was assigned to Coast Guard operations centers where the adventures continued with daring rescues, arresting fugitives, and being on watch during the "Perfect Storm." On September 11, 2001, I was working as a Chief Warrant Officer and marine inspector during my final tour. The world changed that day, and my role in the subsequent War on Terrorism was to lead armed boardings of in-bound ships.

As with any organization made up of people, there was plenty of professional drama throughout my twenty-year career. I encountered some individuals who had slipped through the cracks and didn't belong in my idealistic notion of the Coast Guard. And even though my car was once vandalized, most likely by fellow crewmembers; even though I was once pulled out of my job and forced to work as a personal assistant for a senior enlisted person; even though I was once banished and escorted off base by order of the commanding officer, I never lost that spirit of gratitude I gained upon graduating from boot camp.

Throughout my career I struggled with what my place in the Coast Guard should be. I always felt I should be doing more in a position of leadership. I considered going to Officer Candidate School or being an enlisted Officer in Charge. I decided I wanted to become the skipper of a Coast Guard patrol boat. There were constructive disappointments along the way, and although I never did go to Officer Candidate School or get command of a patrol boat, I was never discouraged. The disappointments just caused me to alter course. When one of my guys died of brain cancer, I started down a new path I could never have imagined, a path that ultimately led to me leaving a lasting legacy on the Coast Guard.

You see, joining the Coast Guard wasn't the only dream I had as a child. As a boy, the sound of the bagpipes marching up Fifth Avenue every St. Patrick's Day caused a mysterious sense of exhilaration in me. At the age of thirty-two, I found a guy in the Coast Guard who taught me how to play. Bagpipes soon became a big part of my life. When one of my guys, who at this time was still living with terminal brain cancer, asked me to play the bagpipe at his retirement ceremony, I started the process of having Coast Guard bagpipers officially recognized and incorporated into the organization. I ultimately founded the U.S. Coast Guard Pipe Band, which is still going strong today with over 150 members performing at over seventy Coast Guard related functions annually. In 2008, I led the third column of the U.S. Coast Guard Pipe Band up Fifth Avenue, through my old neighborhood, in the St. Patrick's Day Parade.

If I had been made the Commandant, it would not have meant more to me than being the Founder of the U.S. Coast Guard Pipe Band. Following a passion, recognizing a talent, and being able to leave an imprint are extremely rewarding experiences, especially when the odds are stacked so highly against an individual. The value of accomplishments is relative and personal. It's not necessary to make millions or to be the leader of the free world in order to gain satisfaction and have a positive impact on the world.

CHAPTER / 1

Boot Camp

"Step up to the platform! Step to the edge of the platform! Cross your arms over your chest! Step off the platform!" The first pair of recruits went plunging into the pool. The smell of chlorine was strong as we stood single file by the stairs leading to a big metal platform projecting out fifteen feet above the pool. "Step up to the platform! Step to the edge of the platform! Cross your arms over your chest! Step off the platform!" Off went the next two.

It was January 1983. I had made it known that I enlisted in the Coast Guard a few months after graduating high school the year before. My friends' parents had made bets on how many weeks I would make it through boot camp before being sent home. I suppose the odds weren't bad. After all, I was about thirty pounds overweight, I was nonathletic, and I never swam a stroke before in my life. I can't explain why I didn't doubt myself.

Most of the recruits thought going to the pool during boot camp was recess, a break from push-ups and sit-ups. But to a handful of inner-city black kids and me, the pool was a real nightmare. The instructors would determine which of us could not swim after watching each of us almost drown.

Despite our fear of the water, our terror of the drill instructor was stronger. Or maybe it was sheer determination. In any case, none of the non-swimmers hesitated. One of my fellow "swim failures," a young black female, sank quickly out of sight. We waited. She didn't resurface for what felt like an eternity. How could she survive? Surely the instructors were going to save her? After all, this is the Coast Guard. She finally broke the surface in a mad panic. She was gasping for air when our instructor pressed a very long aluminum pole to her chest. She instinctively pulled on the pole and the instructor let it slip through his hands— she sank beneath the surface once again. He pulled her back up screaming, "I said never pull on the pole!" Then he towed her back to the side of the pool and she climbed out of the water, still trying to recover. The drill instructor simply ordered her to get to the back of the line.

This series of events disconcerted me as I drew closer and closer to the front of the line. I guess some people thought it was ridiculous that anybody would have joined the Coast Guard without knowing how to swim. I don't remember being scared, only nervous. After all, I had a calling.

For me, being in the Coast Guard was a dream come true. As the son of a New York City subway conductor, growing up in a small apartment in a six-story, walk-up tenement, I didn't have much. We didn't have a shower, washer, dryer, TV, or car. Everywhere we went, we had to get there by subway or bus. It was my mother's job to keep two sons and one daughter occupied and out of trouble. For recreation, my mother came up with many different day trips on mass transportation. One of my favorites was to take the Second Avenue bus down to the South Street Seaport. This was during the 1970s, and New York City was very different from what it is today. The Seaport reeked of dead fish from the Fulton Street Fish Market next door. There were more one-eyed alley cats on the streets than people. The hundred-year-old brick buildings were all abandoned except for one nautical junk store and one museum shop. Pier 17 was old and rotten, and the holes were big enough to fall through if you weren't careful. The pier had three museum ships tied up: an old 325-foot square-rigger named *Wavertree*, a smaller fishing schooner *Letti G. Howard*, and the *Ambrose Lightship*. I grew up playing on those ships on a regular basis and dreaming of what it would be like to go to sea one day—I really wanted to be a salty sailor of the seven seas.

When I was a child I also chalked up a great deal of sea time on the Staten Island Ferry, since that was one of our more exciting weekend family outings. I never sought cover from the wind during those half-hour voyages, regardless of the weather. The cool, drizzly days of spring and fall were best. I loved the feel and smell of the sea air whipping on my face. Whenever the ferry crossed the harbor toward Staten Island, I wondered what it would be like to one day turn left, go under the Verrazano Narrows Bridge, and head out to sea. These ferry rides introduced me to the Coast Guard early on—each trip meant passing the Governor's Island Coast Guard base on the way to Staten Island.

In 1976, the year of the big bicentennial Operation Sail in New York Harbor, I was twelve years old. Of course, my family and I were there watching the parade of tall ships from the Battery. After the parade, we headed over to Pier 17 South Street Seaport and waited in line for hours to take a tour of the *Eagle*, the Coast Guard Academy's sailing ship. The *Eagle* is a 295-foot barque with masts 150-feet-tall. We finally got on board. I thought it was the coolest ship in the world and dreamed of what it would be like to go to sea on such a fine ship.

As my high school years came to a close, it was time to make a decision. I had been in the Boy Scouts and the Knickerbocker

Greys Cadet Corps. I grew up watching WWII movies, reading military histories, and playing with toy soldiers. The military was definitely in my blood. My grandfather served as a constable in the Royal Irish Constabulary during the Irish War of Independence, and my father had been in the U.S. Marine Corps. I didn't have to think too long about which branch of the service to join, as I was most drawn to the Coast Guard's seagoing tradition and lifesaving mission.

"Step up to the platform!" It was my turn to climb the gallows. God help me.

"Step to the edge of the platform!"

"Cross your arms over your chest!"

"Step off the platform!"

Like the others, I complied without hesitation and then I sank, and sank, and sank. I had never been in water over my head. All I wanted to do at that point was to make it back up to the surface and the safety of the side of the pool. I finally broke the surface and thrashed my way to the side of the pool without the assistance of the pole. Mission accomplished. *One step at a time.*

My recruiter had bought me a one-way ticket on a Greyhound bus to Coast Guard boot camp in Cape May, New Jersey. What a way to leave town, through the Port Authority bus terminal of the early 80's. Even Penn Station would have been a step up. My arrival was uneventful. Some young Coast Guard people picked me up from the bus station in a government car and said very little to me or to each other. When I arrived, I was told to wait in a big room full of tables uniformly arranged with sets of gear. I stood in front of the set of gear I was directed to and waited in silence. I was the only one there. I would find out the next day from another recruit, a clueless young preacher-man from Alabama, that I had missed all the fun. The rest of the recruits were flown into Philadelphia airport and were picked up by a Coast Guard bus. In the "squad bay" during a moment of down-time, the former preacher-man explained what happened with a high-pitched southern accent and a sense of outrage, "Well, my goodness, I could not believe it. I thought they were going to say, welcome to the Coast Guard, glad to have you . . ."

"You missed it, man," said another recruit joining in, "as soon as the bus stopped at the front gate he came on and stood at the front, and stared at us. Then he starts screaming at the top of his lungs, 'You dirt bags have got twenty seconds to get off this bus and get formed up, and nineteen of them are gone. Move, move, move!'"

"Oh, my goodness," said the Alabama preacher-man, look-ing down and shaking his head as he walked off. Even reliving the incident was proving too much for him.

The squad bay was a long, narrow room with heavy iron bunk beds aligned in two rows. There was a center aisle and the lockers were against the wall. Since I had never had the oppor-tunity to travel farther than 300 miles from my place of birth, I enjoyed meeting different characters from all over the country. The guys shared stories of their former lives that ended a week prior. It seemed like a lifetime ago as we sat around on the floor in between the rows of iron bunks trying to figure out if a spit shine was supposed to be done with saliva or phlegm. There were former high school football players who weren't the least bit intimidated by the physical training. There were cocky, loud guys from North Carolina, an assortment of inner city Blacks, and Hispanics, and even one guy who bragged about how much money he had made as a male prostitute. We all stopped shin-ing and looked up to see if he was serious. He was. We could only hope he wouldn't make it through the eight weeks into our Coast Guard. He didn't. Neither did two-thirds of the guys we started out with. The Coast Guard was very selective. They had their own entrance exam, separate from the other four branches of the military, and boot camp weeded out anyone who couldn't "get with the program."

It was too hard to make our racks as perfectly as required, so we all slept on top of our tight racks with hospital corners; we wore our army green utility jackets for warmth. It was winter in Cape May, New Jersey. At zero-six-hundred, the company commander would come in and yell, "All right you maggots, fall out now! Let's go, let's go, let's go!" We had just enough time to jump off the rack, put on our boots, and run to formation outside for "morning cals."

"Jumping jacks, begin!"

"Sir, one, Sir! Sir, two, Sir! . . ."

I was not very good at the workouts, but I never gave up. When I arrived at my push-up limit, I would continue to lift my body up from the floor as far as I could and hold it until all of me began to shake and my arms gave out. As soon as my ribs slammed into the deck, I pushed myself up as far as I could and did it again. I knew if I stayed down I would be on the next bus home. Although I wasn't in the greatest shape, I think the instructors appreciated my perseverance. Sometimes, I even surprised myself at what I was able to do.

"Next up! Climb the rope and touch the ceiling, now."

I didn't hesitate when ordered to climb the knotted rope suspended from the very high ceiling of the gym. I just kept going up and never looked down. I was very surprised when I was able to touch the ceiling and get back down without incident.

"Get over here, let's go!" yelled a boot-pusher to a recruit doubled over by the retracted bleachers grimacing for mercy.

What a crybaby, I thought to myself. He kept bellyaching with his hands on his knees. We were not allowed to talk, but it just came out. "Get over here!" I yelled quietly to the belly-acher. I was embarrassed that one of my fellow recruits could not endure the crucible like a man, and I didn't want any of us to give up. The kid rejoined us, but was eventually sent home weeks later.

I wrote detailed letters home to my mother twice a week, sometimes two or three pages long. Shortly before I went to boot camp we had gone to see the movie "Officer and a Gentleman." I loved the movie and hoped Coast Guard boot camp would be similar. It did not disappoint, and my appreciation was reflected in the letters I wrote my poor mother with quotes such as, "Before I crawl up your ass and explode!" Or, when my zipper was found open during sit-ups, "What the fuck! Are you trolling for queers, boy?!"

Near the end of week one, the company commander was supposed to pick one of us to be the leader. They called the position an "RC," which stood for recruit coordinator. Our company commander still hadn't made a decision.

We had to memorize our ten general orders, such as: I will never leave my post unless properly relieved. We were all lined up against the walls outside of our squad bay, when the company commander would walk up to one of us and yell, "What's your sixth general order!"

"Sir, I don't know, sir!"

"Get down and give me twenty!" He meant all of us. We had to become a team. If one screwed up, all got punished. This went on for a while with none of the recruits being able to answer the general order quiz. We had been told to memorize them when we arrived. It was now my turn.

"This is the sorriest bunch of fuck ups I have ever seen!" He stopped in front of me. "How about you, Gilheany? What's your fourth general order?"

"Sir, my fourth general order is . . ." I went on to recite my fourth general order. The company commander was surprised, as he was about to tell us to get down again.

"Oh, is that so? Would you like to try another?" He went on to make some threat about the punishment my mates would receive if I was wrong, just to raise the stakes.

"Sir, yes sir!" I yelled back without hesitation.

"Okay, what's your eighth general order?"

"Sir, my eighth general order is . . ." and I went on to recite my eighth general order.

He did it once more and realized I knew all ten by heart.

"Why is it that Seaman Recruit Gilheany knows all of his general orders and none of you dumb asses knows a single one?! Get down and give me twenty!"

When he was done with us, we filed past him and back into the squad bay. When I passed, he said, "Hey, Gilheany, come here."

"Sir, yes sir."

"I'm going to make you the RC. Here's what the job entails . . . Hey, wait, you're a swim failure, aren't you?"

"Sir, yes sir."

I had not passed the swim test.

"Never mind, you can't be the RC. But I want you to start a study group and teach these dumb asses how to study, OK?"

I was happy to have been singled out for a position of leadership within one week of joining the Coast Guard, even though it turned out I wasn't qualified for it. I was happy to be able to help my fellow recruits with my memorization tricks. I learned early on everybody has their talents, limitations, and individual roles to play.

Swim failures were given two weeks to pass the swim test. The test lasted five minutes. Swim one hundred yards, and then tread water for the remainder of the time. Touch the side of the pool, you start over. While the rest of the company went to the gym to "get cranked" (do push-ups), the swim failures, six other inner-city kids and me, went to the pool for swim practice. One day, while making my way across the pool, one of the instructors was waiting for me at the far side. He yelled, "Come here!" I climbed out of the pool fast and snapped to attention in front of him.

"Sir, yes Sir!"

"Do you want to go home to your Mama, boy?"

"Sir, no Sir!"

"If you don't get back in that pool right now and swim right, I'm going to put you on the next bus back to your Mama! Do you understand me, boy!?"

"Sir, yes Sir!" I hollered as I hustled back to the other side of the pool. Of all the things that he could have said, he chose the one thing that would terrify me the most. All I could think of were the bets that were made back home on what week I would step off the Greyhound as a failure. I could not allow this to happen. I got back in the pool and swam for my life. The instructor decided to have mercy on me and spared me a trip to the bus station.

Every few days at the pool we had to step up on the platform, cross our hands over our chests, and step off. Each time I made it a little farther, but never more than thirty yards or so, as I always got water in my nose and instinctively grabbed the side of the pool. One day I realized if I was going to pass this test, I would have to come up with a new strategy. I realized I needed to swim far enough away from the side of the pool so that when I got water in my nose I couldn't grab the side of the pool. It worked! On the tenth day of boot camp, as the rest of Oscar Company 114 watched from the bleachers, I finished the hundred yard swim.

Now all I had to do was tread water correctly for another two minutes or so. This was no easy task. My mates sat silently and watched from the bleachers while the instructor hovered over me with the long pole. After what felt like hours, the instructor simply said, "Get out."

All I could think was that, after all this, he may have decided my treading water was not up to par and decided to fail me. I had never considered questioning an order before and never did again (in boot camp), but I couldn't help myself. "Did I pass?" I asked, still treading for my life. I must have sounded pitiful. His head snapped around and he gave me a look, with wild eyes and flared nostrils, like you would imagine a drill instructor would give when his order has been questioned by a recruit. Then I saw him check himself.

"Yeah, you passed. Now get out."

The company cheered spontaneously and received no punishment for it. It was one of the proudest moments of my life and one of my biggest accomplishments. Without passing that seemingly small test, none of the rest could have happened.

I felt very sorry for the rest of my boot camp swim failure colleagues, as none of them were ever able to pass the swim test, and they were all eventually sent home.

During the final weeks of boot camp we had what was known as "galley week." The entire company had to work for the cooks, cranking out three squares a day for the entire base. It was the first time you could move from point A to point B without marching to cadence. I guess it seemed like a school field trip.

We were assigned to different stations. Some of us manned the chow line and yelled at the new recruits as we dished loads of food onto their prison trays. The rule in boot camp was, you didn't have to take every type of food offered, but whatever food you allowed to be slapped on your tray had to be eaten. I learned this the hard way, as I had to force myself to swallow a heap of a strange inedible vegetable known to the southerners as "collard greens."

My fun on the chow line didn't last long. I remember being pulled off the line and told to clean a grill in the back of the galley. When I saw this grill, I was horrified. It was worse than any greasy spoon diner grill I had ever seen in Manhattan. But the real scary part was that I knew that when they said, "clean the grill," they wanted to be able to see their reflection in it when I was done. At least, that's what I assumed their expectation was.

I had always been a hard worker. I don't know why. I'd like to attribute it to some sentimental memory of what "My Daddy once told me . . ." as the southern boys do, but that would be a lie. I simply got to work. I scrubbed it with all of my might, for a long time. When I was finished, I found the cook who had set me to the task. He couldn't believe I had gotten his grill that clean. He gathered up a bunch of other cooks to see what I had done. They were truly pleased and amazed.

I had no idea what was going to happen next. The "divil-in-me," as my Irish mother would say, just wanted to get back to the chow line and continue to share this newly discovered green food with more unsuspecting recruits arriving from the north. That's when one of the cooks put his arm around me and said, "Have I got a job for you."

He led me to another grill; there were three or four as I recall. At this grill one of my fellow recruits was struggling with the "steel wool under a bacon press" method of scrubbing. I was immediately disappointed in this fellow, not because he was struggling, but because he had no shame in showing it. After two or

Me on my stoop in Manhattan after boot camp, March 1983.

three scrubs, he would grimace and hold his bicep for us. Lucky for him, the cavalry had arrived and his bellyaching had paid off. He was quickly relieved of his duties, and I was assigned to make a mirror out of his grill as well.

I was nineteen years old, and I was confused about whether I should feel honored, or like a sucker. I must admit, as I looked up from the grill and saw the guy I had relieved horsing around as I scrubbed, I started to feel more like a sucker. But for reasons I can't explain, those feelings quickly passed as I tried to make this grill even shinier than the last. Which I did, and the next one, and the next one.

Graduating from boot camp was one the proudest moments of my life. I experienced a new sense of accomplishment and gratitude. It was the beginning of a great adventure, and those feelings of great accomplishment and gratitude never faded.

CHAPTER 2

402 Lives Saved

After graduating from boot camp, I spent a week at home proudly walking around my old neighborhood in dress uniform, then I was off to Quartermaster and Signalman schools. Because of my pre-enlistment test scores, I had qualified for a guaranteed school after graduating from boot camp. I was given a choice of a few enlisted ratings, or trades. I can't remember any of the others, because once I saw there was an enlisted rating for navigation, I thought no further about it. Not to be confused with the Army supply guys, a Quartermaster in the Coast Guard and Navy stands watch on the bridge and does all the navigating, which includes taking sights of celestial bodies with a sextant to find the ship's position. This was certainly the "saltiest" rating of all.

I didn't join the Coast Guard to become an electronics technician. Who cares about learning a marketable skill? I joined the Coast Guard to be a salty sailor of the seven seas. In my mind, navigating around the ocean with a sextant, a chronometer, a set of tables, and knowledge of the long mathematical calculation would put me in an elite group of sailors from ages past. What could be better than that?

Each school was six weeks long at the U.S. Naval Training Center in Orlando, Florida. After five months of training, I was ready to receive my orders and head out to sea.

In 1790, the United States was in its infancy, and it did not possess a Navy. The Secretary of the Treasury at the time, Alexander Hamilton, recommended a bill to Congress for the construction of revenue cutters to enforce the customs laws of the United States. On August 4, 1790, the bill was signed into law and authorized the construction and equipping of the first ten revenue cutters. This law established what would become known as the United States Revenue-Cutter Service. The modern-day Coast Guard traces its origins back to the Revenue-Cutter Service and celebrates its birthday each year on August 4. The Coast Guard cutters of today perform many of the missions they inherited from their predecessor agency.[1]

"A new boat for a new boot." That was how I was told my new duty station was going to be the Coast Guard Cutter *Bear*, home-ported in Portsmouth, Virginia. She was the first of the Famous Class of medium endurance cutters being built by the Coast Guard in the early 1980's. At 270 feet long, she lacked sheer, that sleek curve of the hull which gives a vessel "nice lines." Despite her boxy, modern profile and snub-nose bow, I still found her an impressive sight when I reported aboard. Her hull was all white with the exception of the distinctive red and blue racing stripes on either bow and the words "U.S. Coast Guard" painted in large black letters on both sides of the hull. Up forward on the snub-nose bow, she was armed with a three-inch, 76 mm cannon covered in a round, grey, fiberglass shell with the barrel of the gun sticking out. Back aft was a flight deck for a helicopter with a retractable hangar. She had a crew of 110 and was fitted with the latest electronics of the day. She was state of the art, especially for the Coast Guard, which at the time was still operating many WWII-era vessels. Her mission was to patrol the Bahamas and Caribbean Sea in search of drug smugglers and desperate Haitian migrants trying to reach the U.S.

Unfortunately, the *Bear* was in dry dock at the time at the Coast Guard yard in Baltimore, Maryland. My going to sea was going to be delayed for a while, until my chief realized I needed some sea time if I was going to be of any use. He had me transferred for temporary duty to the Coast Guard Cutter *Gallatin*, a 378-foot cutter home-ported at Governor's Island, New York. It was quite possibly the same ship I toured as a Boy Scout at the age of twelve. As I got underway for the first time from Governor's Island, I realized we were taking the same route I had taken many times before on my way to Staten Island on the ferry, except this time we would not be stopping at Staten Island. We finally came left, sailed under the Verrazano Narrows bridge, and headed out to sea. It was a bittersweet moment—I thought about leaving my family in Manhattan behind me. I thought about all the adventures that lay ahead of me.

The *Gallatin* was not like the *Bear*. The *Bear* was strict and squared away. Reporting aboard the *Gallatin* was like entering another Coast Guard. People were drinking while the ship was underway, openly worrying about an upcoming urinalysis, and there were rumors of males and females hooking up on board. There were morale nights underway where crewmembers could purchase two beers a piece. Of course, some guys didn't drink. So guys who did, such as myself, ended up with six packs. We once approached a suspected drug smuggling vessel while having one of these morale events on the forecastle.

On the way back to New York, after two months chasing drug smugglers and Haitian migrants around the Bahamas and Caribbean, the Captain called for a dress blue inspection on the flight deck. Many of the crew's uniforms looked like they had been stored in a ball at the bottom of their locker. One fat cook across from me in the ranks could only button the top button of his dress jacket as the rest of it flared open, exposing his enormous belly. When I returned to the *Bear*, the guys could hardly believe the stories I shared. But as it turns out, the guys on the *Gallatin* would have the last laugh.

Seamen recruits in boot camp start at a pay grade of E-1. I was an E-2, seaman apprentice quartermaster. Soon after reporting aboard the *Bear*, before most of the crew knew my name or had a chance to assign me one, one guy asked, "Where's that new guy, Bill?" "You know Bill, Bill Haney?" "Bill-the-Cat!" And so that was it, I was Bill the Cat, named after a comic strip of the time, based upon a misunderstanding of my last name.

While underway, I spent a great deal of time practicing my newfound passion.

"Stand by to mark."

"Mark."

"Thirty-seven degrees, 24.2 minutes."

I called it out slowly as I carefully read the elevation of the sun from the micrometer drum of the sextant. My shipmate marked the time on the stopwatch while I lowered the heavily filtered sun to the horizon and rocked the bottom of the sextant in an arch, carefully tweaking the micrometer drum. This was no easy task to do correctly. Each tenth of a minute of arc, or nick on the micrometer drum, would be equal to one nautical mile when plotted on the chart: there was not much room for error. I suppose this would be tricky enough while standing on land, but from the rolling bridge wing of our Coast Guard cutter, forty-seven feet above the sea, celestial navigation was truly an art form.

Unfortunately, you can't use celestial navigation when it's overcast; you have to rely on other forms of navigation. During one such overcast week, we transited from Bermuda to the Bahamas with regrettable consequences.

"Quartermaster, what's your recommended course to regain track?"

"Recommend a course of 2-4-5, sir."

"Helmsman, come right to course 2-4-5," ordered the conning officer.

"Come right to course 2-4-5, aye, sir," responded the young seaman at the helm.

We had just finished a port call in Bermuda, and it was time to get back on patrol. We were due to rendezvous near the Bahamas with the Coast Guard Cutter *Gallatin*. I thought this was an interesting coincidence, since I had been on the *Gallatin* just a few months before. The track line was a straight shot across open ocean. A front moved in, and soon the sky was 100 percent overcast for days. We were disappointed that we would not be able to partake of our hobby of "shooting" stars and sun lines. It was more than a hobby, of course. It was required. A navigator's day's work, as it is traditionally referred to, includes fixing the ship's position by sight reductions of the sun, as well as morning and evening stars (you can only shoot them at twilight when you can see both the stars and the horizon). There was no global positioning system (GPS) available at the time. We had an electronic navigation system known as LORAN-C, when it was available. Unfortunately, LORAN-C had dead spots, not unlike cell phones in rural areas today. We were in one of those dead spots.

Since this was a new ship, it had all the latest equipment, including the Magnavox Satellite Navigator, or SATNAV, which no one on board had ever used before. This was the system that allowed us to navigate by satellite before the GPS system was fully operational and available. Sometimes we would go five or six hours without getting our latitude and longitude from a good satellite fix.

Unfortunately, this machine also did "dead reckoning," that is, when a satellite fix is received, the latitude and longitude read-out continues to tick away because the course and speed are fed into the machine electronically. This gives you the hypothetical "best guess" as to where you are. Someone above my pay grade decided this was our best position and we should use it as our primary source of navigational information. It was a bad idea. Unbeknownst to us, as set and drift moved us off course, the machine continued to show us proceeding down our intended track. No one was familiar with the machine, or the fact that we had to manually update the position readout when a fix came in. As a result, it was throwing out the good fixes and we didn't know it.

Traditionally, the junior quartermaster always has the four to eight watch, which is 4:00 until 8:00 both in the morning and in the evening. Since I was the junior quartermaster, I had the misfortune of having the "4 to 8 watch" on the morning of the intended Bahamian rendezvous with the other cutter.

As the sun rose, the Captain made his way to the bridge. We established communications with the *Gallatin* on the HF (long range) radio and took down their latitude and longitude. The Captain wondered why we didn't have them on radar or why we couldn't reach them on shorter range VHF radio.

"Quartermaster, plot this position!"

The conning officer called out the latitude and longitude the cutter had passed on the HF radio.

"How far away are they?" the Captain barked.

After being very careful to plot the position correctly, I foolishly announced, "Four miles, Captain."

The conning officer knew right away something was wrong and immediately turned to the clearly aggravated Captain for his reaction. No response was required; he knew what to do and quickly headed for the chart table. I was too young and inexperienced to realize that if we were four miles away, we would have been looking at the other cutter on the horizon. The Captain turned away struggling to keep his cool and tried to explain our delay to the cutter over the HF radio. After a few minutes, with the conning officer and navigator working feverishly over the chart, I was ordered by the conning officer to "lay below."

Wait, could this really be happening? I was getting thrown off the bridge? I walked slowly down the aluminum ladder and past the ship's offices and shops. Any break in routine on a ship that small is noticeable, so my shipmates probably wondered where I was going. I walked aft through the mess deck anticipating what I was about to tell the guys down below in "Ops lounge." I walked down the ladder to the operations department berthing area and into the lounge, a ten-by-ten room with a built-in couch, a built-in table, and a few loose chairs with strings hanging down from the bottom to secure to the deck in heavy seas. The room was packed with guys waiting to start the work day.

"What are you doing down here, Bill? You haven't been relieved. Who's on watch?" said one of the operations department crew.

They all got quiet in anticipation of my response. They knew something was up and were downright giddy about the possibility of hearing some good scoop.

"I got thrown off the bridge," I told them trying to remain cool. I was in disbelief that it had happened, and at the same time I enjoyed telling the scoop just as much as they enjoyed hearing it. I wasn't really ashamed of myself. After all, I was brand new to the Coast Guard and I was simply an E-2 doing what I had been told. There were three other quartermasters and four officers far senior to me who had also been involved in this debacle.

I explained to the guys that we were lost, and that there must be a problem with the SATNAV. I told them I had been ordered to lay below and that the officers were currently trying to figure out where we were. My shipmates were in disbelief, but excited by the drama of it all.

One quick-witted gunner's mate put his hand on my shoulder and, shaking his head in disbelief sighed, "Bill the Cat." Then, almost immediately, he raised his head displaying an evil grin, proud of his spontaneous comic inspiration, he declared, "Bill the Un-Sat-Nav-Cat!" to a roar of laughter.

Good grief! Un-Sat?! I wasn't used to being referred to as unsatisfactory. It was like when we named the cook who served us raw chicken "Salmonella George."

We eventually rendezvoused with the *Gallatin* later that day. Thank God we were in open ocean, or our navigational error could have been disastrous instead of just embarrassing. I would later run into the quartermasters I sailed with on the *Gallatin*. They had a great time telling me how much fun they had that day imagining me on watch, and getting the *Bear* lost. I was on track to have a reputation as a buffoon. I had been thrown off the bridge, the guys on the *Gallatin* knew about it, and I had been given a hilarious nickname to make it stick.

No one was fired or sent to the brig for this incident, but I'm sure there were repercussions for those senior to me. Believe me when I tell you, this lesson was not lost on us. We mastered that SATNAV and much more. From then on, we were required to follow *Dutton's Nautical Navigation*, the traditional navigation textbook, to the letter. Even though I was technically the least to blame as the junior man, I took this embarrassment to heart. I was not only embarrassed for myself but for my shipmates as well. I was also somewhat disappointed in my more experienced superiors. The navigation team had let the Captain down and embarrassed him in front of the senior officer on the other cutter. While I had a great deal of respect for my lieutenant and chief, I resolved never to solely rely on others. This was never going to happen to me again. A couple of years later, I would learn just how important this lesson was.

"Captain, I have the message board for you," said the radioman as he made his way between the chart table and the helmsman, to the Captain in his Captain Kirk-style chair. Shortly after the Captain read the message board, and discussed it with the conning officer on watch, I was given a position to plot on the chart. The report stated two overloaded Haitian sailboats in danger of sinking had been sighted, and we were directed to proceed to the scene at best speed.

During this time, there was a steady flow of Haitian migrants headed for the U.S. in all kinds of unseaworthy crafts. Many of these desperate people would have to sell all of their possessions in order to pay unscrupulous boat owners for passage. Their chances of a successful voyage were slim. The sea claimed its share of those vessels we weren't able to catch or save. We had picked up many before during my time on the *Bear*, and returned them to Haiti. Some people had been caught and returned by the Coast Guard two or three times.

The latitude and longitude I plotted turned out to be on the tip of the "Tongue of the Ocean." The Tongue of the Ocean is an area of deep water in the middle of the Bahamas, surrounded by islands and shoal waters. On the chart, the shoals are shown in blue and the deep water is shown in white. The Tongue of the Ocean looks like a big white Rolling Stones tongue, and these Haitian sailboats were just south of the tip of the tongue, in the dangerous blue shoal area.

There was only one way for our 270-foot cutter to get close, and that was to go right down the Tongue and see how close we could get without running into the rocks. A Coast Guard aircraft confirmed the report and explained the situation was worsening. The wind and seas had picked up and both vessels, overflowing with poor Haitian men, women, and children, appeared to be sinking.

"Helmsman, come to course 1-8-0, all ahead full!" was the command.

"Come to 1-8-0, all ahead full aye, sir!"

It took a while to get down the Tongue and I had the four hour watch prior to us getting on scene. Unfortunately, once again, the LORAN-C electronic navigation system was not dependable in the Tongue and the SATNAV satellite navigation system was not due to give us a good fix for five or six hours. I plotted our last good satellite fix and dead reckoned our course and speed meticulously for hours. Dead reckoning is simply estimating your current position via arithmetic. The formula is: Distance = Speed x Time. The margins for error are due to wind and current, effects commonly referred to collectively as "set and drift."

The real payoff for a meticulous navigational plot came when you finally got a fix and you plotted it, and it would land right on top of your dead reckoned position. I always took great pride in my navigational plot, and this time was no exception. As the hours passed, I worked like a surgeon on the chart with my compass and dividers, accounting for all the course and speed changes.

As we got closer to the tip of the Tongue, and the dangerous shoals, the Captain came to the bridge. We snapped to attention with a hand salute.

"Captain on the bridge!"

"Carry on," the Captain replied as he made his way to the chart table.

Ships don't usually go down into the Tongue. There's no reason to. It's not a shipping lane and there is no way out for a ship of any draft except to go back up the way it came in. In that sense, it was kind of a spooky place. The Captain was justifiably concerned.

"What time do you have us on scene?"

"1730, Captain."

"When was your last fix?"

"Four hours ago, Captain."

The Captain was silent. He didn't like that answer. We were required to plot a fix every half hour, but dead reckoning was all we had to go by. As we got closer, the apprehension built. The Captain was relying on my dead reckoning. If I was wrong, we could run up on the rocks at a full bell. The Captain reduced speed to a two-third bell, juggling the need for prudent navigation with the need to get on scene before the darkness and weather would make this massive rescue operation even more difficult than it was already going to be. Some time passed as the Captain considered the options. Then it occurred to him, "What time do you have us crossing the one hundred fathom curve?"

I wasn't ready for that question. I hadn't even thought of it. But he had been going to sea for about twenty years, and I had only been at sea for two. I found where the one hundred fathom curve crossed our track line on the chart. I put down the dividers and carefully measured the distance. Then I did the math and replied with conviction, "Minute seventeen, Captain."

That was military jargon for seventeen minutes after the hour. The pressure was on. The Captain was going to judge the accuracy of my plot based on how closely I calculated when we would cross the one hundred fathom curve. If I was off, he would have no confidence in our position and would have to pull back and perhaps even abort the mission rather than put the ship in danger. The sun was setting and this rescue could not be done safely at night. If we had to delay our arrival, chances were the sinking vessels would not stay afloat until first light. We had to get there and get this mission accomplished before dark—many lives depended on it.

The fathometer shows the depth of water beneath the keel and was mounted on the forward bulkhead of the bridge above the windows. All eyes were on the fathometer, which showed no reading. The deepest reading the fathometer could show was one hundred fathoms and we were in water much deeper than that. No one spoke as the minutes ticked away. You could feel the tension. I was confident in my plot, but I knew the margin for error was quite large due to the course and speed changes, and the effect current and wind could have on the ship.

Suddenly the fathomer started flashing.

After a few more flickers, the fathomer set itself on a reading of seventy-three fathoms. The Captain and everyone else on the bridge immediately spun around to see the clock on the aft bulkhead of the bridge.

It was exactly seventeen minutes after the hour.

"Very good," the Captain said to me with a smile. Then he turned to the helmsman, "Helmsman, all ahead full!"

"All ahead full aye, Captain," the helmsman replied.

It wasn't long before the water changed color as we proceeded into the shallows. We were so far away from where a ship should be that we saw the jagged rocks just a short distance ahead, protruding from the sea. Eventually we had the sailboats in sight, too. They were about forty feet long, fifteen feet wide, wooden, with tree trunks for masts. There was very little freeboard on these sailboats they were so overloaded. The people on deck were packed so thick they were hanging over the rails. We would later learn there were approximately 150 people on one boat and 250 people on the other. I would not have believed this was possible had I not experienced it firsthand.

It was starting to get dark, and the wind and seas had picked up. The overloaded boats rocked precariously in the swells. We could tell by the commotion of people as we approached that they wanted off those rickety boats, now. This was no interdiction operation; this was going to be one hell of a rescue.

We immediately launched both small boats: the motor surf boat and the rigid hull inflatable. The first small boat made a

Haitian sailboat, which contained 150 people in the Bahamas, 1980's.

pass around one of the sailboats to assess the situation, but when the small boat came within ten feet of the sailboat, a bunch of terrified Haitians leaped for it, all of whom fell into the choppy seas. It became apparent rather quickly that many of these people could not swim—our small boat crew worked feverishly to pull them out of the water as fast as possible.

I was watching with binoculars from the bridge wing of the ship, when I saw one person break the surface of the water well behind our small boat and immediately disappear beneath surface once again. We radioed our small boat and notified the coxswain of the drowning person behind them. The coxswain brought the boat around fast and yelled at the leading seaman.

"Jump!"

"What?" replied the confused seaman.

"Jump, now!" yelled the coxswain.

The coxswain was a grouchy old bearded boatswain's mate. But there was no one else you would have wanted in charge of this rescue. He had spent his career operating Coast Guard surf boats on the treacherous bars of the New England coast.

The leading seaman immediately jumped into the sea and dove beneath the surface. He came back up with the drowning Haitian boy and quickly got him into the small boat. "How cool was that!" I thought as I watched from the bridge wing above, meticulously block printing the dramatic account in the ship's log. Some part of me wanted to be down there, too.

Having recovered all the Haitians from the water, the small boat headed back to the ship with the first load. The Haitians were so desperate to get off of those sinking sailboats they continued to leap into our small boats as soon as they came within range. This would continue on into the evening with both boats shuttling boatloads of Haitians back to our flight deck.

When it was over, we had rescued all 402 souls from those two sailboats, and they were all on our flight deck. Our crew was outnumbered four to one. I suppose if they wanted to, the Haitians could have taken over the ship and driven it to Miami themselves, but they were just happy to be alive.

The cook made a concoction he called Haitian stew: oatmeal and ground meat, mixed together in a large metal garbage can. We wanted the people to have an opportunity to clean up and remove the uncomfortable sea salt covering their bodies. Having 400 people running around inside the ship using our showers and facilities was unmanageable. So the shower consisted of hosing the people down in small groups on the fantail. We even had a jail on the bow for the few troublemakers who needed to be separated from the rest.

We eventually made it back to Port Au Prince, Haiti, and turned the 402 individuals over to the Haitian Red Cross, safe and sound. Many of us had mixed emotions about returning these poor folks to their misery. It seemed there should have been some "A for effort" clause in the law, where you got to come to the U.S. after such a desperate and noble attempt. Oh well. There was nothing left for us to do except pray for them. I had been to Haiti thirteen times during those early days of my adulthood, and the abject poverty and the compulsion of these folks to escape their home left a lasting impression on me.

Our leading seaman received the Coast Guard Commendation Medal for his heroic rescue, an unusual occurrence for a junior enlisted man. But there was nothing usual about this event. We were all very proud of him.

It occurs to me that if I had not accepted my spot in quarter-master school, then I too would have been a non-rated seaman and possibly under the command of the salty coxswain during this rescue. How would I have performed given my marginal

We were better at saving boats than sinking them.

swimming ability? I know that drowning Haitian boy was much better served with that leading seamen coming to his aid than me. The salty coxswain and the leading seaman were right where they needed to be that day. It turns out that Bill the Un-Sat-Nav-Cat was right where he needed to be, too.

It was a great honor to be in the business of saving lives. But I realized early in my career that those in peril on the sea were not the only ones who needed saving.

CHAPTER 3

A Rough Start

"You fucked up this time, Bill."

I realized I was not alone as I started to come to. The tiny lounge was full of my operations department shipmates. Some were sitting at the round table inches away playing cards, some were standing around the table, or leaning on the walls. I was fully clothed, but sprawled out on the orange pleather sofa, embarrassed. I propped myself up on my left elbow to face everyone. My embarrassment quickly gave way to the symptoms of a severe hangover.

It was ten o'clock on Sunday night, September 16, 1984. The lounge was full because married guys who didn't live on the ship would come aboard Sunday night to be ready for a regular workday on Monday morning. It was the usual in-port routine for the Coast Guard Cutter *Bear*.

"Bill the fucking Cat, you drunk motherfucker," said the gunner's mate, shaking his head with a hint of amusement to hide his underlying concern. I tried to hide mine as well, but I wanted to know how I had "fucked up this time" without appearing vulnerable.

I smiled and said nonchalantly, "Why, what happened?" as if it didn't bother me.

By now I was sitting up in my usual, former New York street hooligan attire: jeans, a flannel shirt, an Eisenhower jacket and white, low-top Converse. My head was pounding.

"You got booked!" said the gunner's mate. Most of the rest of the guys in the crowded room ignored this exchange. They were less concerned about me and probably figured it was about time. After all, who wants to live with a drunken fool who can't even make it to his rack? I knew this was more than the usual banter I received for my youthful indiscretions; this was serious.

"What happened?"

"The *Point Huron* was sinking at the dock and we couldn't get your drunk ass up!"

I had been out on Saturday night, some special occasion. Someone had bought a keg to celebrate, and we were in some park in the Portsmouth, Virginia, area. Although I had tried to control my intake for quite some time, and had fooled myself into thinking I could, the seemingly endless flow of beer from the tap got the better of me. A shipmate had driven me back to the ship around four o'clock in the morning. Being from Manhattan, I didn't drive. Single guys like us lived on the ship in a tiny berthing area with twenty-one racks stacked three high. I had landed on the couch in the lounge and passed out. Now that I had emerged from my alcohol-induced coma sixteen hours later, the gunner's mate and a few others filled me in on the rest of the story.

At 7:00 a.m., the *Bear's* quarterdeck watch-stander received a report that the Coast Guard patrol boat *Point Huron* was sinking at the dock. Since it was the weekend, all the other Coast Guard ships at the base had only duty crews on board. The rest of the crew, including me, was on liberty. The watch-stander on the quarterdeck sounded the alarm, "Away the Rescue and Assistance Team!" The duty section sprang into action, grabbing their individually assigned equipment from the repair locker, and after mustering on the flight deck, hustled down the dock to pump out the *Point Huron* before it sank.

The Officer of the Day was a young ensign, and standard routine was to have all personnel on board, on duty or not, muster on the flight deck to be used as needed. After a half-hearted attempt to wake me, my operations department shipmates mustered on the flight deck. When asked for reports, they reported, "all present or accounted for, except for Gilheany." The young ensign understood, but told them to get me up on deck.

They tried everything from pouring water on my face, to picking me up and watching me fall back down. I remembered none of it. They eventually gave up and returned to the flight deck without me. The young ensign gave a report to the operations officer who told the ensign to place me on report, or "book" me, which he did.

In those days drinking was part of the routine. You didn't get in trouble for drinking; you got in trouble if it affected your ability to do your job. Being able to drink hard without it affecting your work was seen as a quality of a good sailor. It was the one quality of a good sailor I did not possess. Sobriety was an actual category on the enlisted evaluation form; the lowest mark you could get in any category was a one, and the highest was a seven. I would get fives and sixes in all categories except sobriety, for which I would get a two.

"Oh well," is all I could say as I made my way to the berthing area to undress, climb in the rack, contemplate my sins and prepare for their consequences.

My mother, God rest her soul, bought me my first can of beer when I was eleven years old. It was St. Patrick's Day and she thought it would be a nice gesture for me and my thirteen-year-old brother to have one can of beer each. I remember the deli we went into on East 82nd Street in Manhattan to pick it out. She meant no harm. Drinking and drunkenness was part of her reality, although she never drank herself. Her father drank heavily his entire life, and she married a man who drank even more than her father.

When I was about six years old, I was walking with my mother, brother, and sister up Third Avenue between 81st and 82nd Street. We lived around the corner in a six-story, rent-controlled, walk-up tenement. Yorkville had not yet been transformed into the Upper East Side and the old buildings and neighborhood businesses had not been replaced with the luxury high-rise apartment buildings of today. We had just left Mrs. Herbts' German bakery and were in front of Falk's drugstore when my mother turned to gather the three of us up and said, "Quick, let's cross the street."

I had no idea what had brought this on. After all, there was nothing across the street that was part of our routine. I was curious because my mother's sudden urgency felt out of character. I looked ahead on the sidewalk and saw a few men out in front of the Breffni Arms, a neighborhood Irish bar. It was not uncommon to see Irishmen drunk and falling down out front, and occasionally, some were even passed out and sprawled across the sidewalk. They did it in style, too. Back then they all wore inexpensive dark or gray suits and ties, all the time. I noticed that this was one of those days where a drunk was laid out on the sidewalk; passing pedestrians walked over and around him. As we stepped into the gutter between cars to cross Third Avenue, I turned my head once more to look at the drunk in the suit passed out on the sidewalk. It was my father.

My father didn't live with us. My mother had gotten a restraining order before I was a year old. He lived in rooming houses in the neighborhood and would come by every Thursday night with his subway conductor pay. My mother would cook him dinner, and we would sit at the tiny Formica kitchen table like a real family. My father always finished first and would treat us all to a dessert of unfiltered Pall Mall smoke. He was a nice man when he was sober. But the sheet metal door of apartment 18 bore dents from the nights when he would try to kick it in during one of his drunken rages. On the other side of that door: my older seven-year-old brother, armed with a Louisville Slugger, my mother, armed with her broom and rosary, and my sister and I cowering behind them.

By the time I was thirteen, I was drinking heavily every weekend. My over-protective mother could no longer control my fifteen-year-old brother who begged for his freedom. She had decided to turn him loose and me along with him, and put it all in God's hands: a dubious strategy for child rearing, no doubt. By the time I was fifteen, I was drinking every day and getting blasted every weekend. I was designated a "Juvenile Delinquent" by the New York City Police Department not once, but twice.

There was a gang of us, all Catholic schoolboys from Irish families. We met every Friday and Saturday night on the corner of 84th Street and Lexington Avenue and would raise hell throughout the neighborhood. Although we never referred to ourselves as the 84th Street Gang, everyone else did. The drinking, while it got me into plenty of trouble growing up, never really bothered me. I had big dreams and would talk about them with my friend Dennis on Sunday nights after evening mass while sitting on a stoop drinking the final quart of beer of the weekend. I would talk about how I was going to join the Coast Guard as soon as I graduated from high school. I knew I had to get out of town. I couldn't bear the thought of living any longer in a 500-square-foot apartment with a family of large people, two dogs, and two cats. It never occurred to me that my problems would follow me.

I thought only of the possibilities available to me once I got out of that environment.

As soon as I graduated, I went to see the Coast Guard recruiter. A few months later I was off to boot camp. I made it through boot camp but I resumed my drinking habit afterward and had my first alcohol related incident while in Navy Signalman School. I continued to rack up alcohol-related incidents while serving on the Coast Guard Cutter *Bear*. Each time I would get in trouble for a drunken incident, I would be counseled by my bosses. They cut me several breaks because I was an excellent performer otherwise. After a while, though, I started to realize I had a problem. I tried to cut back. I would only drink three or four beers a night, and I was proud of myself when I skipped a day without a drink. But feeling good about my ability to control my drinking was short-lived. Inevitably, there would be some special occasion and, despite my best efforts, I would get drunk and in trouble once again.

The incident involving the sinking of the *Point Huron* at the dock on September 16, 1984, would be my thirteenth alcohol-related incident in only a year and a half in the Coast Guard. The next day, my immediate supervisor and drinking buddy gave me the lowdown.

"This is serious. You have been placed on report. You're going to have to cut down on your drinking. They're going to send you to NASAP."

NASAP was the Navy Alcohol and Substance Abuse Program. It was where sailors got sent who were determined to have a drinking problem or a DUI. It was also the first step before sailors who continued to drink would be processed for discharge from the service. I had to go see my executive officer next.

The executive officer said that while we had had this conversation before, this was it. He had placed me on the waiting list for the next available slot at NASAP. He must have dispensed with the charge sheet, because I received no punishment for the offense. I was a difficult case for them. I was well liked and a top-notch Coast Guardsman in all aspects except for my drunkenness.

But I was not relieved. I knew I deserved punishment for the offense. I was ashamed of myself. I was so proud to have achieved my childhood dream, to make it into the Coast Guard, and I was about to blow it all. All the other times I had gotten into trouble I was able to use the excuse, "Yeah, but at least I am excellent at my job." Now I failed to respond to a sinking cutter. I had no solace. The desire to fulfill my dream was only slightly stronger than my desire to be drunk, but the pain of the shame I was feeling was overwhelming. I believe that desire to succeed made me desperate enough to want to quit drinking: I knew I couldn't do both. It was only when I wanted to stop drinking bad enough, when I admitted I could not control it, and when I surrendered myself to the grace of God that I was able to quit. And by the grace of God, I never drank again.

My mother was a devout Catholic. Some would say to the point of religious dysfunction. She had a small library of religious books, and our apartment contained many religious statues and pictures. We said the Rosary together as a family and went to daily mass. She prayed constantly. Though it may have been flawed, her faith and devotion had a profound effect on me. My mother taught me a prayer called the *Memorare* that was particularly helpful during this time. I said it constantly, for many years:

> Remember, O most gracious Virgin Mary,
> that never was it known,
> that anyone who fled to your protection,
> implored your help,
> or sought your intercession was left unaided.

> Inspired with this confidence I fly to you, O Virgin of
> virgins, my Mother,
> to you I come, before you I stand, sinful and
> sorrowful,
> O Mother of the Word Incarnate
> despise not my petitions, but in your mercy, hear and
> answer me.

By giving me my first beer, my mother may have provided me with the catalyst for my addiction. But it was also my mother who inspired in me what I would need to stop drinking: faith. I had faith in God and in myself. I believed if I tried hard enough and asked for God to help with the rest, that He would, and He did. Thanks be to God.

I never went to NASAP; there were too many Navy guys with DUIs who took priority. I did it cold turkey. It was not easy. I was still on a ship calling on many Caribbean ports, with the same guys I was used to going ashore with to get blasted. I knew I had to fill the void with other things to occupy my time and keep my mind off the temptation. I made my first list of things I wanted to accomplish and bought a camera to substitute my habit with a hobby.

I got my first driver's license at the age of twenty-one. At the end of my first year of sobriety, I had saved over $3,000 and had lost sixty pounds. I bought my first car, a 1975 Oldsmobile Delta 88 convertible. It was huge and red and had two big, red leather couches. I spent lots of time washing and waxing that car or working on it in the auto hobby shop.

I went home to New York a few times after I quit drinking and hung out with the old gang. I would drink a few Cokes as they consumed the usual six packs. It was awkward for me and them. I soon realized that drink was the glue bonding us to-gether, that all of my glue was gone. So, after a couple of trips home on leave, I came to the realization that if I was going to succeed, I was going to have to move on and leave those guys behind as well. So I did.

For the first seven or eight years I would occasionally wake up terrified that I had taken a drink, only to realize it was the same recurring nightmare. It got easier after that. Of course the addition of a few motivating factors helped. I met my wife in my third year of sobriety, for instance, and she would never tolerate a drunken fool.

My father eventually quit drinking too, and we ended up having a good relationship. I never held any of it against him. After all, we all have to live life with the hands we are dealt, even if the deck is stacked against us. I interviewed him for a family history documentary I was making only six months before his sudden death in December 1993. During our talk, he voluntarily admitted, "If I was asked what was the biggest accomplishment of my life it would not be what I did, but what I stopped doing."

I have accomplished a good deal in my life, and I try not to dwell on it, but I know what was true for my father is also true for me. I pray I will never forget that.

CHAPTER 4

Adventures On The High Seas

Built in Tacoma, Washington, the *Bear* was brought through the Panama Canal to the East Coast by her crew of "plank-owners." Plank-owner is a term for a ship's first crew who, according to nautical tradition, were supposedly entitled to claim their plank from the ship upon decommissioning. This term originated when ships were made of wood, but it still escapes me why anyone would want to do such a thing.

I was the fifth non-plank-owner to report aboard. The plank-owners had been through a lot getting the *Bear* into operation and were a very proud and tight-knit group. They all had "plank-owner" stenciled across the back of their hats, and they shared great sea stories of the trip around, including one about being smashed by a gigantic freak wave when coming out of San Francisco Bay. I really didn't care about not being a plank-owner, but I desperately wanted to be smashed by a gigantic freak wave. We non-plank-owners could only hope to have our own equally worthy adventures someday.

Being the first of the class, the *Bear* had to go through a great deal of testing and evaluation. One such test involved wiring the ship with many sensors, getting underway in search of the worst weather we could find, and then running octagonal patterns to see how the ship handled being hit from the seas at different angles. This kind of testing was done by a division of the Navy known as the David W. Taylor Naval Ship Research and Development Center. This division of the Navy was named after Rear Admiral David Watson Taylor, a naval architect and engineer who served as Chief Constructor of the U.S. Navy during WWI.[2] The David Taylor engineers came aboard, set up their racks of equipment in one of the shops on the main deck before running wires all over the ship.

"I need the chart of Cape Hatteras."

The ship's navigator was getting ready to lay the octagon track lines for our testing run, and they had chosen the waters off of Cape Hatteras, North Carolina. This area is known to mariners as the "graveyard of the North Atlantic," due to the number of ships lost there over the centuries. The Captain was excited a low pressure system was moving in to ensure the severe conditions the engineers were hoping for. I was excited as well, and looked forward to earning my sea legs.

As we approached the area off Cape Hatteras, the skies were 100 percent overcast, the winds were blowing a gale, and the seas were huge. In addition to navigation, one of my duties as the Quartermaster on the bridge was to log the weather. I was conservative with my estimates of sea height, as there was no way to measure it. The Captain made an unusual visit to the chart table, looked at my weather log, and before walking away he simply said, "those are thirty-foot seas."

The usual seasick crewmembers were already incapacitated by the time we encountered the heavy waves. At the end of each leg of the octagon, I had to announce that leg's completion and that crewmembers should fill out the corresponding survey

Quartermasters on the *Bear* before the 1986 ban on beards, from left to right: Joe Gispert, the author, Joe Spillman.

forms in their workspaces. The questions on the survey forms included questions like, "Did you vomit? How much did you vomit? Were you incapacitated? Were you able to complete your assigned duties?" As soon as I completed the announcement and put down the microphone, I looked down the four-step ladder from the bridge to the passageway below in front of the watch-stander's head. There were guys losing their most recent meals in the bathroom while other, less fortunate souls were stuck in the passageways. They were left to vomit into garbage cans, because the scuttlebutt, or water fountain, was already overflowing with cascading puke. *Only seven more legs to go . . .*

Almost no one ate, and almost everyone walked around with a black garbage bag tucked in their belt just in case. By the grace of God I was immune to this cruel affliction. I enjoyed the monstrous seas and felt like an old salt. While these thirty-foot seas would be the highest I would ever experience, they would not stack up to being smashed by a gigantic freak wave. But good things come to those who wait.

About a year later, we were on a drug patrol down in the Caribbean. The trade winds are prevailing winds out of the east down in those lower latitudes. They were named the trade winds because they conveniently blew the sailing ships from Europe and Africa to the Caribbean for trade back in the days of sail. During this particular day the wind was blowing hard, and whenever the snub-nose bow of the *Bear* faced easterly (into the wind) it tended to crash into the waves, not cut through them. The sea spray would occasionally reach the bridge windows, which were forty-seven feet above the surface.

The Captain noticed that one of the yeoman or storekeepers ("passengers" as we called them because they stood no watch) was at the doorway of the bridge waiting to take pictures of the waves crashing up forward. The Captain disapproved and told the officer on watch, "Tell him to lay below." At the next "quarters" on the flight deck, he explained to the entire crew mustered there that these weather conditions were nothing special, and that they would be the normal operating conditions for the *Bear*.

A day or so later, the seas had built significantly and we were heading right into them. With each swell the ship would climb up to the crest, then crash down into the trough. The spray was hitting the windows on every swell. The Captain decided to film the *Bear* navigating these seas to document how she handled.

"Get the duty ET up here with the video camera." Shortly thereafter, the duty ET (electronics technician) arrived on the bridge with a big, TV-crew-sized video camera. He was told to take position in front of the bridge console directly behind the center window. The waves continued to crash against the windows as the ship pitched violently up and down.

The chart table on the *Bear* faced aft. I was leaning over it and working on my logs. The Captain and the XO (the Executive Officer who was second-in-command) watched out forward.

"Oh, it looks like this is the one we've been waiting for, XO."

I immediately turned around to look out the forward windows. A wall of green water blocked out the sky and spanned my entire field of view: it was headed straight at us. I leaned forward to look up. I could see the crest of the massive wave; it was even with the flying bridge on the deck above us.

"Yes, sir," said the XO.

The XO and the rest of us instinctively grabbed hold of the nearest rail to brace for shock. Then our ship crashed into this green wall while traveling at approximately fifteen knots. She came to a complete stop and shook violently. Due to the severe pitch from being engulfed by this fifty-foot wave, the front of the ship was underwater and the propellers back aft were out of the water, which caused the severe vibration. Fiberglass dust from the drop ceiling panels rained down on our necks. As the bow started its way back up to the surface, the windows looked as if a straight-stream fire hose was trained onto each pane. We couldn't see anything. The vibrations subsided as the propellers settled back into the sea, and the water on the windows receded, as if the fire hoses were slowly shutting off. The bow continued to rise. By the time we could see outside, all we saw was another wall of water just as big as the last.

Bam!

Once again the ship came to a complete stop and shook violently. Two freak waves in a row was a rarity, but our gallant ship powered back out of this second wave, and the water on the windows gradually cleared.

"Oh look, we lost the jack."

The Captain noticed the jack staff, the flag pole on the bow of the ship used for flying the Union Jack in port, had been snapped off at its base and was hanging over the side.

"Um, Captain . . ."

The XO, looking concerned, pointed down to the snub-nose bow.

The Captain leaned forward. He almost had to press his forehead to the window glass to get a good look at the bow.

"Shit! Helmsman right fifteen degrees rudder, all ahead one third."

"Right fifteen degrees rudder, all ahead one third, aye sir."

The Captain steadied us on an easier course and slowed the ship to conduct a damage assessment. After I logged the helm commands, I moved forward to see for myself. The lifelines around the deck perimeter (three courses of taut cables held together by a series of stanchions) were either completely gone or hanging over the side. The fire station on the forward bulkhead was gone and the engineers claimed the forward bulkhead was set in an inch or two from the impact. But the most obvious and most severe damage was to our 3-inch, 76mm gun mount. The entire port side of the fiberglass shell covering the gun mount was torn off and hanging like a broken egg shell. All of the electronic innards on the left side of the gun were exposed. The gun's 3-inch shells were stored below deck in the ammunition magazine, and that space was now flooded with three feet of water.

The engineers did an excellent job of damage control and pumped out the flooded magazine. They made temporary repairs to the gun mount to make sure no more water got in. But that was the end of our drug patrol. After the damage was reported back to our operational command, the ship received orders to proceed to Roosevelt Roads Navy Base in Puerto Rico for repairs. After a couple of weeks in Puerto Rico, the *Bear* was back in business.

While the incident and resulting damage were unfortunate, I suppose it provided the Coast Guard with more valuable data about what this class of vessel could and could not take. But more importantly, at least to this young quartermaster, was that with this experience I had definitely earned my sea legs in addition to a story to rival that of any plank-owner. Now all I needed was a good drug smuggling case to add to my collection of sea adventures.

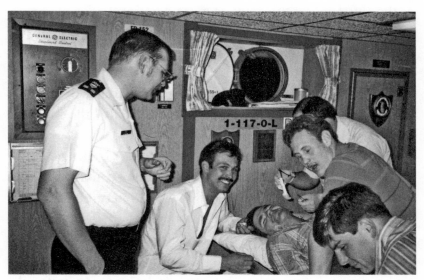

A seaman getting stitches by the corpsman on a mess deck table after a night of liberty in a foreign port.

During the mid-1980's, the war on drugs was in full swing. Many Coast Guard assets were dedicated to disrupting the flow of cocaine and marijuana into the United States from Colombia. Operation Hunter Forces sought to address this concern by disrupting established drug trafficking routes during the winter of 1985 and 1986. Aircraft from the Coast Guard, Navy, and Drug Enforcement Agency would support Coast Guard and Navy ships as they carried Coast Guard law enforcement teams on patrol throughout the Caribbean basin. The hope was that drug smugglers would be forced to take less developed, more visible routes. Intelligence agents from the U.S. and several Latin American countries would then provide communication links between the task force and the intelligence organizations of the participating governments. The Coast Guard Cutter *Bear* was selected to serve as the "nucleus" of this inter-agency operation.[3]

Of course, as enlisted crewmembers, we were kept in the dark about these plans due to concerns about "operational security." After all, someone could always over share with their spouse over the dinner table and that spouse could, in turn, unknowingly mention it to someone connected to the Medellin drug cartel while at the grocery store.

"I have what appears to be a small contact bearing 2-2-0 at 24,000 yards. I haven't been able to determine course and speed yet because the radar signature is weak and intermittent."

"Very well, have combat divert the aircraft to identify the contact."

"Aye, aye, Captain," said the operations officer as he headed to the combat information center below the bridge to personally pass on the Captain's orders. It was not standard procedure for the operations officer to serve as messenger, but everyone understood the importance of this mission and nothing could be left to chance.

"Combat" was the bat cave that required a secret security clearance just to walk in the door. It was dark in there. Radarmen, fire control technicians, and electronics technicians made do with what little light emanated from equipment screens, illuminated console buttons, and status boards. It was from this room that the chief radarman spoke over a secured radio with the Coast Guard aircraft, tail number 2-1-1-3.

"Coast Guard 2-1-1-3, Cutter *Bear*, over."

"Cutter *Bear*, Coast Guard 2-1-1-3, over."

"2-1-1-3, Cutter *Bear*, we have a contact bearing 2-2-0 at 24,000 yards from our current position, request positive ID, over."

"Cutter *Bear*, 2-1-1-3, Roger. Diverting at this time."

As enlisted men, we all held the appropriate security clearance, but we lacked the "need to know" to have access to the classified message board which would have explained exactly what we were doing. So, we had to put the pieces together as we went along and hope that the young officers would fill us in during those long, lonely mid-watches.

It was clear that we were much more interested in this particular radar contact than most, and we usually didn't have Coast Guard jets available to identify radar contacts, which were over the visual horizon. The height of eye from our bridge wing was forty-seven feet, which meant the distance to the visual horizon was four nautical miles. The contact we were tracking was 24,000 yards, or twelve nautical miles, away. So, they couldn't see us and we couldn't see them.

We were in the Caribbean Sea just north of the Colombian coast and this radar contact, we were hoping, was a cabin cruiser loaded with cocaine heading to the Bahamas or United States. This operation required months of planning, as well as embedded intelligence agents on the ground in Colombia who could pass on information regarding vessel departures.

"Captain, Combat reports the aircraft has confirmed that is our contact."

"Excellent! Come to course 2-7-0," the Captain directed the conning officer on watch.

As the ship came to a westerly course, the Captain kept his eyes in the radar hood to make sure we didn't lose the contact off of our port beam to the south. He passed along his orders to the operations officer and the conning officer on watch, "You make sure you have the contact on radar at all times. If you lose track of it you are to call me immediately."

"Yes, sir."

"I want us to stay far enough away from him so he can pass us going north without seeing us. Once he gets north of us I want to fall in behind him while staying well below the visual horizon."

"Yes, sir."

"We don't want to lose this contact," the Captain said deliberately, making sure to make eye contact. "This could be a big one."

"Yes, sir," replied the two junior officers in unison.

The strategy was to shadow the vessel on its northbound voyage, find out the track the smugglers were using, and ultimately board it near the Bahamas.

We maneuvered the ship well out of the path of the suspect vessel and continued to track it as it headed northbound. We fell in behind the vessel just as the Captain had ordered, and were careful to stay close enough so as not to lose radar contact, but also stay far enough away so as not to be seen over the horizon.

Our pursuit continued on for some time. Each relieving watch silently wondered whether the distant, tiny green blip was really still the boat we were supposed to be tracking. What would happen if it turned out to be the wrong vessel? What if the preceding watch lost track and we were chasing a Dominican fishing boat instead? Some officer's career would surely be in jeopardy.

"Looks like he's headed for the Jamaica Channel," the conning officer said to the quartermaster on watch.

"Yes, sir. I have him making good a course of about 0-1-6 true. Do you think he'll stay closer to the Jamaica side or the Hispaniola side?"

"No tellin'. But he'll be headed for the Windward Passage after that. He'll probably stay close to the Cuban side when he gets up there. They probably think most Coast Guard vessels keep closer to Haiti to stay away from the Cuban territorial waters."

"But we'll still be able to track him in there, no matter how close he gets to Cuba. He's got a pretty good radar signature."

"Roger that."

The suspect vessel passed through the Jamaica Channel and continued northbound. Due north of Jamaica is the south shore of Cuba. The shoreline there runs almost due east and west and contains two very important ports. On the east end of that south shore lies Guantanamo Bay, or "Gitmo," as it is otherwise known to Navy and Coast Guardsmen. Christopher Columbus made landfall at this harbor in 1494, and it was seized by the United States during the Spanish American War. The U.S. has held a perpetual lease on the bay since 1903 and since then has operated an important U.S. naval base.[4] All Navy and Coast Guard vessels operating in and around the Caribbean go to Gitmo for fuel, and it was well known to the crew of the *Bear*.

Another important harbor on Cuba's south shore, Santiago de Cuba lies forty miles to the east of Guantanamo Bay. It was discovered by the Spanish in 1514 and served as the launching point and base of operations for expeditions by explorers such as Hernando Cortez and Hernando de Soto.[5] It is also the site of

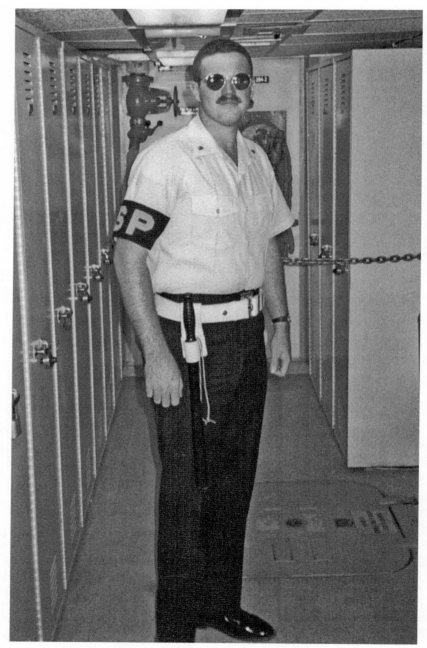

Duty at Guantanamo Bay included shore patrol.

the Battle of San Juan Hill where Col. Theodore Roosevelt led his Rough Riders to a decisive victory.[6]

"I don't show him coming right yet. He looks like he's heading due north to Cuba instead of the Windward Pass."

"Maybe he just wants to get closer to the Cuban coast before he turns right."

We continued to track the suspect vessel as it entered Cuban territorial waters and continued on toward the Cuban coast.

"Quartermaster, make sure we don't get into Cuban waters."

"Aye, sir. On this current course and speed I have us entering Cuban territorial waters at 1336."

"Very well."

We came to all stop and drifted right at the edge of Cuba's territorial sea boundary. We were due south of the entrance to Santiago de Cuba harbor. The suspect vessel also appeared to have come to all stop just a few miles from shore and appeared to be drifting as well. Hours passed. We wondered if they had somehow figured us out—were they tracking us on their own radar? Did they head deep into Cuban territorial waters in an attempt to shake us? After all, we were still mired in our Cold War with the Soviet Union during the winter of 1985, and the U.S.S.R. maintained close ties to Cuba. The suspect vessel must have known we could not pursue them into Cuban waters.

"We have a very large contact on radar coming out of Santiago harbor, sir, and heading straight for us. I have it constant bearing decreasing range."

"I heard they have a secret Soviet naval base in there," offered one of the bridge crew to add to the drama.

"They're probably wondering what we're doing sitting outside of their harbor."

"Quartermaster, make sure we haven't drifted into Cuban waters. I don't want an international incident."

"Aye. I have us one mile south of the boundary, sir."

"Very well. Keep a close eye on the set and drift."

The officer of the deck called the Captain to the bridge.

"Captain on the bridge!" I called out as the Captain stepped up onto the bridge. We all snapped to attention with a hand salute.

"Carry on," said the Captain as he headed over to the radar. The bridge was crowded by the routine, three-man watch, the Captain, the Executive Officer, the Operations Officer, and the assistant Operations Officer. "Get the EMO up here," ordered the Captain. Soon the electronics chief warrant officer joined the bridge's ranks.

"The contact is closing fast, still constant bearing, decreasing range."

"Very well," replied the Captain quietly.

The officers got very quiet and started scanning the horizon ahead with their binoculars. Soon a large, grey ship appeared on the horizon heading straight for us.

Every mariner knows the standard procedure for avoiding a collision in this type of situation. A crewmember picks up the VHF radio and calls on channel 16 saying something like, "Vessel off my starboard bow heading due south from Santiago, this is the United States war ship off of your port bow, channel one-six, over." But that never happened, and we never received such a call. The big, grey ship just kept coming at us, in silence.

The officers stood in a row pressing their binoculars against the forward windows, each trying to determine what kind of a ship was coming at us, and what this ship's intentions might be. The Electronics Warrant Officer broke the silence.

"It's a Soviet . . . ," he said, rattling off some official designation. Everyone else either knew what he was talking about, or pretended to. I asked, "What kind of ship is it, sir?"

"It's a Soviet spy ship."

The bridge was extremely quiet once again as the Captain pondered whether he should pick up the radio and call the approaching ship, but he kept that quandary to himself. We hovered around the radio waiting in silence for the ship to call us, like we were in a horror movie waiting for the phone to ring. The only sound came from the officer manning the radar: he called off the yards as the distance closed, "Three thousand yards, two thousand yards, one thousand yards, five hundred yards, four hundred yards, three hundred yards . . ." We started to make out that there were people on their bridge wing. We all started to move outside to our bridge wing. They were dead slow ahead as they approached, and their bridge wing was full of Russian officers and crewmembers. Soon they were close enough that we could see their faces without the binoculars. They circled around us 180 degrees. No one waved. They just looked at us, and we looked at them. They completed their pass around us and headed right back toward Santiago harbor. They probably just wanted to make sure we were not a U.S. spy ship.

"Do you still have the contact?" asked the Captain, worried that it might have been lost during the encounter.

"Yes, sir. It's bearing 3-4-7, at 14,000 yards."

"Very well. Let me know if he starts moving again."

"Aye, Captain," replied the Officer of the Deck, as the Captain and other officers were lying below.

A few more four-hour watches passed, and our suspect vessel remained in the same general vicinity. We maneuvered at a slow bell making sure to never put our stern to the vessel, which might allow it to escape through a radar blind spot. Most ships have their radar antenna mounted on the forward part of the mast. This means that the mast blocks the radar directly astern of the ship. There are a few degrees of arch, directly astern of a ship known as the radar blind spot where other vessels might not show up on radar.

"Looks like he's making way!" said the young conning officer on watch.

"Let me have a look," said the quartermaster as he took a turn on the radar and watched the green blip start to move slowly eastward.

"Captain, he looks like he's on the move again. I show him on a course of 1-0-0 at eight knots. Looks like he's headed for the Windward Pass," said the young conning officer over the bridge phone to the Captain below in his cabin.

"Very well, call me when he gets to the Pass, and don't lose him."

"Aye, aye, sir."

We tracked the contact through the Windward Passage and on into the Bahama Islands. Luckily they stayed in waters deep enough for us to follow. Eventually they headed into a tiny harbor in a small Bahamian Island. We took up station in international waters, below the radar horizon.

"They probably went in for fuel and supplies," said the operations officer.

It was nighttime, during the 2000 to 2400 watch, and as always, the bridge was totally dark to ensure the watch-stander's night vision was not compromised. After sunset on a ship, all interior lighting is switched over to low-level red lights, which do not affect night vision for the watch-standers. Quartermasters needed some light to do chart work, so the chart table was equipped with a desk-type lamp with a low-level red light. To keep this light from interfering with the rest of the bridge crew's vision, a curtain hung from a ceiling track, covering an area just slightly larger than the chart table itself, and was kept closed all night.

The Captain suddenly appeared inside the chart table curtain, which was an unusual occurrence.

"Let me see your pencil."

"Yes, sir," I said as I handed the Captain the pencil and moved out of his way.

The Captain proceeded to draw a figure eight-shaped track line pattern on the chart right over our current position. He also drew arrows on the track lines to indicate the direction he wanted us to follow, so that we wouldn't confuse it with the reciprocal, 180-degree opposite course. He explained that following this pattern: heading directly east toward the island, then turning left 130 degrees north-northwesterly, then back due east toward the island again, and so forth, that we would be able to maintain position without ever having our stern and radar blind spot toward the island. I suppose the Soviet encounter led him to believe a ship drifting just raised too much suspicion. He reiterated the importance of running the pattern exactly as he had laid it out. At midnight my watch was over, and after being properly relieved, I laid below for some shuteye.

At 0730 I returned to the bridge to relieve the watch and assume the 0800 to 1200 watch. As I checked the chart and the log, I couldn't believe my eyes. This 0400 to 0800 watch had been running the figure eight pattern in the opposite direction almost their entire watch. Our stern and blind spot had been towards the harbor entrance for hours and we couldn't be sure the suspect vessel didn't get away.

"Mr. Jones, can you come here for a minute, sir," I said from the chart table.

Mr. Jones was a young ensign. He was not a Coast Guard Academy type, but an Officer Candidate School graduate. He had graduated from a university in Tennessee where he played football, and he didn't always grasp why things were "such a big deal."

"What's up?" he said as he leaned over the chart table on both elbows.

"The Captain laid out this track line last night and you were supposed to run it in this direction," I said as I outlined with my finger the intended track the Captain had drawn on the chart. "See the arrows he drew?"

"Oh, well, we missed a turn so I just came about and decided to do it in the opposite direction," he said, not understanding what the big deal was. I explained to him why the Captain had drawn the pattern the way he did, but Mr. Jones still didn't get what the big deal was.

"Oh," he said, laughing goofily as he did while walking away, glancing back at me to see if I was going to continue to make a big deal of it.

I stood there staring at him in disbelief with my mouth open as he resumed his position leaning on the front of the radar on the opposite side of the bridge. Then he decided he should at least get the ship going in the proper direction before someone else found out.

"Helmsman, right 10 degrees rudder, come right to course 0-9-0," Mr. Jones told the helmsman in the nonchalant manner of a guy who was not too concerned about anything other than getting in his rack after the dreaded four-to-eight in the morning watch.

"Well, are you going to tell the Captain?" I said.

He looked at me like I was crazy and said, "No," still laughing it off.

"But sir, the suspect vessel could have gotten away while you were headed away with your stern to the island."

"Ahhh," he groaned and waved his hand at me to go away, and looked back and laughed nervously.

"Sir, you have to call the Captain and tell him. He's going to find out one way or another."

Mr. Jones was no longer laughing. He found me to be an extreme annoyance, and he really didn't see the big deal.

After a few more attempts to reason with him, I said, "Well, sir, if you don't call him, I will," as I held the bridge phone in one hand and held down the connector with the other, offering him one last chance to do the right thing.

He stared at me for a few seconds, wanting to punch my face in. Then he said, "Give me the phone," grabbing the receiver out of my hand.

He held the handset for a few moments of silence, stared out the window, and rehearsed what he would say in his mind. Officer promotions were extremely competitive, and he dialed the Captain knowing this call could mark the end of his career. The Captain appeared on the bridge a few moments later.

"Captain on the bridge!" I called out as we all snapped to attention with a hand salute.

"Carry on," said the Captain as he made his way over to Mr. Jones and his watch relief.

The Captain was not happy, and after a discreet expression of his displeasure, Mr. Jones laid below having been properly relieved. The operations officer was next in line to experience the Captain's displeasure and was expected to bring about a solution. The decision was made to request a Coast Guard Falcon jet from Air Station Miami to fly over the harbor and confirm the suspect vessel had not gotten away. The mood was somber on the bridge and the tension was thick. After all, the quartermaster on watch had screwed up, too, by not catching Mr. Jones' error, and none of us felt good about the errors of our shipmates. If this vessel got away after all this, it would be a real disaster. A few hours passed. Finally, the Combat watch-standers reported they had the Falcon's radio guard. It wasn't long after that we received the good news.

"Captain, the Falcon confirmed the suspect vessel is still moored at the marina."

We were all relieved. You could hear an audible sigh. We continued running the Captain's pattern a while longer.

"Captain, I have a small contact coming out of the harbor entrance. The radar signature looks like our guy."

"Very well. Let's come about and head away from the island to a point at which we are both far enough away from the island where we can come about and intercept the contact before he has time to get back into Bahamian waters."

"Aye, Captain. Helmsman, come to course 2-7-0."

A few hours later, after the calculations were made based upon our top speed and the average top speed of a cabin cruiser, the point was decided upon where we would come about and intercept the suspect vessel. When we reached the point, the conning officer reported to the Captain.

"Captain, we are ready."

"Very well, set the law enforcement bill."

"Aye, Captain. Quartermaster, set the law enforcement bill."

"Aye, sir."

With that, the quartermaster pulled the ship's announcing system microphone out of its holder and made the long awaited pipe, "Now, set the law enforcement bill, set the law enforcement bill, boarding team Alpha lay to the armory."

The crewmembers on boarding team Alpha headed to the ship's armory to dress out. They donned their body armor and Beretta 9mm side arms. One boarding team member would carry the Remington 12-gauge Riot shotgun, and another would carry the M16 rifle. The gunner's mates would mount and man the .50 caliber machine guns on the deck behind the bridge just in case warning shots or disabling fire was required.

"Helmsman," the conning officer said with a bit of excitement and relief, "come right to course 1-3-5, all ahead full."

"Come right to course 1-3-5, all ahead full, aye sir," the helmsman replied with a smile, knowing this long chase was coming to an end.

We steadied up on course and the ship quickly came up to full speed. As we closed on the suspect vessel, the Officer of the Deck called off the range to the suspect vessel, "4,000 yards, 3,000 yards, 2,000 yards." As it came into view for the first time, we could see that it did indeed match the description of our suspect vessel. The conning officer made the approach off the vessel's port quarter.

"Vessel off my starboard bow, vessel off my starboard bow, this is the United States Coast Guard, channel one-six, over."

Silence.

"Vessel off my starboard bow, vessel off my starboard bow, this is the United States Coast Guard, channel one-six, over."

More silence.

We were now very close to the cabin cruiser as they plowed along at full speed through the waves, pretending not to see the 270-foot white ship with guns next to them. The gunner's mates manning the .50 caliber machine guns were hoping the suspect vessel didn't answer. They knew that they would eventually be called upon to fire short bursts in front of the vessel as warning shots, and they looked forward to it.

"Let's give him some more time," said the Captain. "Keep trying to raise him."

"Vessel off my starboard bow, vessel off my starboard bow, this is the United States Coast Guard, channel one-six, over."

"Coast Guard, Coast Guard, *Lady Jane*, over," finally came the Spanish-accented response over the radio.

"*Lady Jane*, this is the United States Coast Guard Cutter off your port quarter, we have some questions we would like you to answer, how copy over?"

"Coast Guard, *Lady Jane*, Roger, Roger, go ahead, over."

With that began a long list of questions known as the pre-boarding questionnaire. All the names of their crew were obtained and run through intelligence databases. The pre-boarding process ended with this request, "*Lady Jane*, U.S. Coast Guard, we are requesting permission to board your vessel at this time."

It is much easier to get a consensual boarding than to go through a vessel's flag state for a statement of no objection, or to have the vessel declared a stateless vessel. After a short delay, the unexpected response came.

"Roger, Coast Guard. Yes, you may come aboard. We will heave-to."

It was hard to determine if it was a good sign or a bad sign when a suspect vessel agreed to a consensual boarding. There was always the possibility of a language barrier, or that the suspect vessel was not aware that they could say "no" to a big white ship with guns. They also could be totally innocent, or they could be trying to play innocent because the stuff was hidden so well they probably thought we couldn't find it.

The boarding team climbed into a twenty-foot motor surf-boat (an open craft designed to right itself if it capsized) that was lowered into the water by davits from the starboard side of the flight deck.

"Boat's at the rail. Boat's in the water. Small boats away."

The master of the *Lady Jane* was directed to muster his crew on the stern of the vessel. The coxswain maneuvered the small boat next to the *Lady Jane* and the boarding team climbed aboard. After the initial security sweep to make sure no one else was hiding on the vessel, the boarding officer began a 100 percent space accountability search of the vessel, which is a long and tedious process to ensure there are no hidden compartments, or fuel tanks within fuel tanks. The boarding teams were very well trained at the Coast Guard Maritime Law Enforcement School in Yorktown, Virginia, and had a lot of hands-on experience.

"Have they found anything yet?" the Captain asked after a couple of hours.

"No, nothing yet, Captain," said the Officer of the Deck.

"I thought for sure this was going to be a good one," the Captain said, disappointed.

A short while later, I heard the boarding officer call over his radio, "Uh, Captain, I think we have something." The Captain headed for the radio. I grabbed the binoculars and headed for the bridge wing. The boarding officer was talking via his hands-free headset from the deck of the cabin cruiser. He faced us with both hands raised and a big smile on his face. Both of his hands, the drill he was carrying, and portions of his face were totally covered with white powder.

After all these hours on the suspect vessel, they had been running out of places to look, but then the boarding officer said he had noticed the fiberglass shower stalls looked new. He decided to take a chance and drilled into the shower wall where he discovered 404 pounds of 90 percent pure cocaine with an estimated street value of $30 million.

The four crewmembers of the *Lady Jane* were placed under arrest and transferred to our flight deck where they were shackled together and placed under prisoner watch. Four *Bear* crew-members, known as a "prize crew," were transported to the *Lady Jane* to take it to Miami under our escort. Once in Miami, the prisoners were transferred to the custody of the U.S. Marshals to await prosecution. While heading back to homeport, we looked forward to our in-port period and felt as if we had made a small dent in the drug trade.

The underway schedule for the *Bear* was usually a month underway followed by six weeks in port. But occasionally, the in-port period had to be cut short in light of events unplanned and unforeseen.

CHAPTER 5

Challenger

A shipmate noticed me putting on my dress uniform while standing at my locker in "Ops berthing."

"Duty blues!"

"Yep. You know who's got the OOD today? I hope it's Mr. Breyer; sometimes he finds a reason to skip the drill."

The crew of the Coast Guard Cutter *Bear* was divided up into three duty sections. This meant that every third day in port, I had duty. The duty section stayed on board overnight and was prepared to respond to emergencies of every kind. On this Tuesday morning, January 28, 1986, I had the 0800 until 1200 quarterdeck watch, which is why I was noticed putting on my dress uniform instead of the usual work uniform.

"No. Sorry. We had Mr. Breyer last night," came the reply from the shipmate, happy to have his duty day behind him and anticipating going home to his family that night.

After a quick breakfast and a couple of cups of coffee, I headed up to the quarterdeck. The quarterdeck is not an actual deck, mind you. It is a place on board a ship which is designated as the reception and ceremonial area of the ship while in port. Our quarterdeck happened to be on the flight deck, just at the opening to the helicopter hangar, which was also where the brow, or gangway, was located. The quarterdeck watch-stander answered the one landline phone, routed calls, made "pipes" or announcements on the general announcing system, and sounded the alarm in the case of an emergency. The quarterdeck watch was also responsible for ringing the Captain and other visiting officials aboard and returning the salutes of all those who crossed the gangway.

It was extremely cold that day in Portsmouth, Virginia, with a low temperature of fourteen degrees—twenty-two degrees below average.[7] Unfortunately for the quarterdeck watch there was no shelter. His desk was an aluminum box lifted up on hinges from the inside of the hangar and was propped up by two makeshift table legs fashioned from aluminum pipe. We were afforded an electric space heater that sat on the flight deck under the desk and served no purpose other than to keep the ink in the government pens from freezing so we could write the required entries in the ship's log. It's a wonder no one was electrocuted from wedging the pens into the space heater wire grating to get the ball point as close to the heating coils as possible. There were always two or three pens jammed in the heater at any given time.

After freezing for a few hours on the flight deck, I looked forward to being relieved for chow. Lucky for me, my relief came up early, around 1130. I expressed my gratitude for his promptness, passed the scoop quickly, and laid below. The mess deck was warm and lively. Everyone was eating lunch and watching the television mounted on the wall in the corner. Then I remembered that today was another space shuttle launch; luckily I hadn't missed it. I grabbed my prison tray and went through the chow line quickly. The countdown began just as I made it to the table and set down my tray.

"Ten, nine, eight, seven . . ."

There was a great deal of publicity about this mission, mostly because NASA had held a competition known as the "Teacher in Space Program." Out of the 11,500 applicants, a teacher from New Hampshire by the name of Christa McAuliffe had been chosen to fly with the other six astronauts on this space shuttle *Challenger* mission. The cold front affecting us in Virginia was also causing great concern at Cape Canaveral, Florida. The temperature there was thirty-six degrees—thirty degrees colder than any previous launch, but this mission had already been cancelled a couple of times for various reasons.[8]

" . . . *six, five, four* . . ."

Unbeknownst to the general public at the time, some project engineers harbored grave concerns over the performance of "O-rings" on the solid rocket boosters in these temperatures. NASA contracted the Morton Thiokol corporation to produce the solid rocket boosters. However, in order to transport the rocket boosters to Cape Canaveral, they had to be made into sections that would fit on railroad train cars. Therefore, the sections of the rocket booster were designed to insert into each other. The connections were critical and were sealed with a double set of rubber gaskets known as "O-rings." These solid rocket boosters were reusable, and after each mission, the engineers would examine the components. An engineer for Morton Thiokol, Roger Boisjoly, had noticed that during previous missions, the O-ring system had come close to failing. Six months prior, he had written a memo warning that in cold weather the connecting seals would fail: "The result could be a catastrophe of the highest order. Loss of human life."[9] Since the extreme cold would cause the O-ring seals to be less pliable and not seal properly, Boisjoly was extremely concerned about this *Challenger* mission and he was trying desperately to convince his managers of the danger and to cancel the launch.[10]

" . . . three, two, one, lift-off!"

I sat down on my swiveling mess deck chair in front of my tray and watched the white smoke billow out across the Cape, and the shuttle slowly start to climb skyward. What I didn't notice was the black smoke shooting out of one of the rocket booster seals indicating that the O-rings had already failed. A conference call had been held the night before between NASA and Morton Thiokol about the O-rings and the danger. Despite the protests of Boisjoly, Morton Thiokol managers gave their recommendation for NASA to go ahead with the launch, and NASA officials made the final decision to go ahead. Boisjoly recalled going home that night and telling his wife that they were going ahead with the launch the next morning and that they were probably going to kill all the astronauts.[11]

The *Challenger* continued to climb as we watched and listened to the standard commentary we had become accustomed to. All appeared to be well until seventy-three seconds after lift-off. In that moment, we wondered if something about this launch was different, but no one wanted to say. A couple of "Oh shits," and "What the fucks" could be heard in hushed tones across the mess deck, but mostly everyone remained quiet waiting to hear what was going on from the CNN announcer Tom Mintier, who was covering the launch. As soon as the vehicle exploded, he stopped speaking and said nothing for the next twenty-three seconds as we all watched the once-skyward smoke trails now spiral back toward Earth. We were still not sure what to make of the images on screen: the seven astronauts, in their crew compartment, were being hurled in a "ballistic arc" to their deaths. Then Tom Mintier reported the rockets had separated apparently as the result of some kind of explosion. A few minutes later the mission control could be heard saying they were taking a close look at the situation, but that it was "obviously a major malfunction."[12]

It was a very quiet meal after that. We stayed glued to the television and waited on more details. But it didn't remain quiet for long. An hour after the explosion the shipmate who had relieved me on the quarterdeck made the pipe: "Now, the brow is secured, the brow is secured. All hands make preparations for getting underway."

Normally, the ship would remain in port for four to six weeks in between patrols. We were not scheduled to get underway for a few more weeks. For single guys like me who lived on the ship, this was a welcome break to the in-port routine. We were getting underway to rescue the astronauts of the space shuttle *Challenger*. We had no way of knowing they had all been killed two minutes and forty-five seconds after the explosion when their crew compartment crashed into the sea at approximately 207 miles per hour.[13]

"The brow is secured," meant that whoever was on board was not allowed to go ashore for any reason. It was a bit of an imposition on married guys who thought they were going home that night, and now would not be seeing their families for a few weeks without being able to say goodbye. Essential crewmembers on leave were recalled. The phone line was jammed.

We headed to the bridge to break out the charts of the Florida coast and make sure they were corrected and up to date. The navigator laid out the track lines and received tasking from our operational controller on the details of the mission. We had been tasked to participate in the massive search, rescue, and recovery operation. Before long, we were en route to the scene of the disaster.

We arrived in the search area on February 2 and began our search. There were many ships, planes, and helicopters from many branches of the military involved in the search. The *Bear* searched over 19,000 square miles of ocean, but we weren't having much luck.[14] Having operated in this piece of the Gulf Stream current for years, and knowing the current could run from four to six knots to the north, we figured much of the debris would be north of our position, but we had been assigned our search areas. Then after a few days we received orders to proceed north. An aircraft had found a debris field, and we were being directed to proceed to the scene and recover the debris.

"Helmsman, come to course 0-0-0, all ahead full."

We were on our way to the reported debris, which was even farther north than we had estimated it might be.

"I have orange smoke bearing 0-3-0, on the horizon, sir."

The lookout had spotted the orange smoke marker which had been dropped into the debris field by the circling aircraft. The guys down below in "combat" were communicating with the aircraft on UHF radio.

"Roger that. Keep an eye on it."

Soon we were vectored alongside the debris by the circling aircraft. We launched the rigid hull inflatable boat from the stern using the articulating crane mounted back aft. The crew of the small boat was able to secure a line to some large pieces, which turned out to be panels from the solid rocket boosters. The panels were subsequently hoisted aboard the back deck with the articulating crane. The *Bear* was not designed for retrieving debris, and the articulating crane's sole purpose was to lower and retrieve the small boat. Despite that, all the debris was recovered without incident, thanks in part to the ideal weather conditions. A number of smaller pieces of what appeared to be insulation were also recovered.

"There's another piece about fifty yards off the port beam."

The small boat was directed to investigate and reported back.

"This is a very large piece; we may not be able to tow it far."

"Very well. Standby."

The conning officer gave the helm commands to maneuver the *Bear* alongside the debris. From my vantage point on the bridge wing it looked large, rectangular, and mostly black. We had no idea what it was. We assumed the astronauts were probably dead at this point, but still thought we might be able to locate and recover the crew compartment with their remains if it was still afloat. In this moment, we weren't giving that much thought, as we were focused on how to get the large piece on board safely. The small boat crew was able to rig a hoist and secure the line to the crane hook. As the crane operator slowly hoisted the piece of debris out of the water and the rest of it slowly came into view. It was a long rectangular piece, which was slightly curved, like a long section of a cylinder. As the crane operator hoisted the piece out of the water, it twisted in the wind and the other side of it became visible. Unlike the convex side which was charred black, the concave side was pristine with sea foam green, plastic pegboard-type paneling. We soon realized we were looking at one of the space shuttle *Challenger*'s cargo doors. It was eerie to see the outside, once a stark white, now burned black while the interior was untouched, just as it had been a week before. The heat resistant tiles designed to protect the orbiter from the intense heat generated by reentry into the atmosphere had clearly done their job.

We secured the debris on the back deck and a seaman was directed to hose off the saltwater to prevent further deterioration. The entire crew eventually made the pilgrimage back aft to check out the debris, instinctively remaining quiet while lining up along the rail of the flight deck to gaze down upon the debris piling up.

We were given orders to deliver the evidence back to Cape Canaveral where it was offloaded under tight security. We hadn't

Recovering Space Shuttle *Challenger* debris off the Florida coast.

The *Bear* recovered panels of the rocket booster and the space shuttle cargo door.

found the astronauts, but we were glad to have recovered a significant piece of the *Challenger*. The vehicle would be reconstructed as part of the investigation—in the end, only 55 percent of the *Challenger* would be recovered from the sea.[15]

The recovery mission continued. On March 7, Navy divers from the Navy salvage vessel USS *Preserver* located the crew compartment and the remains of the seven astronauts on the ocean floor. It is believed that some or all of the seven were alive and conscious until impact with the ocean. It was determined that three of the crew had turned on their emergency air supply and had used two minutes and forty-five seconds of air.[16]

I was unaware of the backstory of this disaster at the time and only became aware of Mr. Boisjoly's struggle years later. The House Committee on Science and Technology established the Rogers Commission to investigate the accident. Boisjoly testified courageously about the events leading up to the disaster. The House Committee concluded the accident was caused by a ". . . failure in the aft field joint on the right-hand Solid Rocket Motor," and that, "neither NASA nor Thiokol responded adequately to available warning signs that the joint was defective."[17] The report goes on to say that "the Marshall Flight Center should have passed to higher management levels the temperature concerns of Thiokol engineers the night before the launch of Mission 51-L."[18]

Despite this Congressional investigation, no one from NASA or Morton Thiokol was held accountable for the disaster. Roger Boisjoly, on the other hand, paid a stiff price for speaking out at the Rogers Commission. He had been shut out of his workplace and was shunned by his former co-workers.[19] He had become a pariah.

The *Bear*, as is customary in the military, received a Coast Guard Meritorious Unit Commendation for participating in the recovery operation. All individual crewmembers received a certificate from NASA signed by NASA Administrator James Fletcher which read:

> In appreciation of your dedication to the critical tasks performed in support of the presidential commission investigating the space shuttle *Challenger* accident. Your valuable contributions assisted in identifying the actions required to return the national space transportation system to flight status.[20]

In its report, the House Committee stated, ". . . The lessons learned by the *Challenger* accident are universally applicable, not just for NASA, but for governments, and for society."[21]

Amen.

Although Boisjoly was not able to save the crew of the *Challenger*, he was undeterred and went on to become a renowned speaker on workplace ethics as well as a lecturer at over 300 universities and civic organizations. He was eventually awarded the Prize for Scientific Freedom and Responsibility from the American Association for the Advancement of Science.

Roger Boisjoly, a kindred spirit who provided the most valuable lessons of all, died on January 6, 2012. The *New York Times* published a lengthy obituary of the unsung, would-be hero. His story put into perspective the award we received for helping cleaning up the mess he fought so hard to prevent.

I spent three years on the *Bear*, and during that time I was able to overcome a reputation for drunkenness and the fact that I had been thrown off the bridge when we got lost. Apparently, others took notice and on my last patrol, I received an unexpected reward from my commanding officer.

CHAPTER 6

Airborne

The rating designator for a quartermaster is a ship's wheel, which is worn proudly on the upper left sleeve above the chevrons. While a quartermaster's primary duties on the ship involve navigation, he is also responsible for conducting helmsmanship training for all non-rated seamen, the guys who would normally man the helm. However, during special evolutions where precision is preferred, the quartermaster with the billet unofficially known as "master helmsman" is required to take the helm. These special evolutions include such nail biters as underway replenishment (when the ship goes alongside a Navy oiler and refuels while moving ahead at fifteen knots) and other more common evolutions such as flight quarters (when helicopters take off or land on the flight deck).

I served aboard the *Bear* for three years. After having sobered up and having recovered from the initial embarrassment of being thrown off the bridge, I had earned a reputation as a squared away sailor. My job during all special evolutions was "master helmsman." I was good at it. After all, I was qualified to steer a ship before I was licensed to drive a car.

"Now, set flight quarters condition one, set flight quarters condition one."

"Great. Why can't they ever do this during my watch?" I thought.

Back to the bridge I went, having barely digested my lunch and with no time to recover from the 0800-1200 morning watch from which I had just been relieved. As I climbed the three steps to the bridge from the "combat" deck below, it was full of the usual commotion associated with "special evolutions." I squeezed passed my quartermaster buddy from Maine who was blessed with the inability to stop fooling around. With his ever present grin, he mumbled some snide remark about Joe, our perpetual victim quartermaster, getting rolled by some whore during the last port call. It was the type of commentary that was customary when we were all present. He was an expert in making sure only his target audience, myself and Joe, heard it on the crowded bridge. It was a fine line for an enlisted man to tread, between living the life of a "drunken sailor" and maintaining the military bearing and professionalism required to do one's job correctly. It was an art we never acknowledged, but were proud to practice just the same. Underneath the constant teasing, each man was sizing the other up, but we were also strengthening an unspoken, brotherly bond.

"Recommend a course of 0-6-0 true, sir, to have the relative wind thirty degrees off your starboard bow," yelled the same Maine-i-ac over the commotion, having expertly whipped out a reverse-true-wind calculation on the maneuvering board using the rolling plotter and dividers with a speed and accuracy so impressive even the Coast Guard Academy grads looked on from the starboard side with envy. He didn't wait to be asked; we all knew what to do, having done this many times over the past three years.

"Whatcha got?" I asked the seaman at the helm. I needed to relieve him of the helm so he could get down below and dress out in a full fire-fighting suit as part of the helo-crash fire-fighting team.

A Coast Guard cutter equipped with a flight deck on drug patrol does a lot of flight quarters. The helicopters and their crews would fly out from Coast Guard Air Station Miami and would be assigned to the ship for a couple of weeks. They were used to flying ahead of the ship and locating suspect vessels to board.

There was a very long waiting list for seamen to go to an aviation school and become part of the helicopter crews. Most guys thought that was the coolest thing they could do in the Coast Guard. I never understood all the hype about helicopters. The thought of it just didn't interest me. Going up in one was never on my radar, not when there were ships to sail.

Quartermasters usually stood two four-hour watches in a twenty-four-hour period. If flight quarters happened to be during your watch, it was no big deal; you simply took the helm and someone else navigated. But, if flight quarters were called while you were asleep in the rack, you had to jump out and get to the bridge fast. Fatigue was not a consideration—it built character.

"Steering 0-6-0, checking 0-6-5; engines all ahead two-thirds."

"Mr. Jones," I said loudly with the fingers of my right hand extended and joined, touching the edge of my visor. Mr. Jones, the officer of the deck, turned and looked at me, raising his hand to return the salute.

"Request permission to relieve the helm, steering 0-6-0, checking 0-6-5; engines all ahead two-thirds."

"Very well," came the response as we both dropped our salutes.

"I relieve you," I told the seaman, who responded, "I stand relieved," and hustled down below to dress out.

"Captain on the bridge!" yelled the Maine-i-ac behind me.

Silence and stillness followed, with everyone frozen in position, the fingers of their right hands extended and joined, touching the edge of their visors. He might as well have said red light, green light, one, two, three.

"Carry on," said the Captain, who, like all senior officers worthy of their position, showed no pleasure in the power he had worked so hard to achieve.

As the Captain eased into his Kirk-like chair, the officer of the deck and other officers were completing the pre-flight checklist.

"Who's taking a ride on this flight?" the Captain asked. This was an unusual inquiry for the Captain to make.

At the time, it was traditional for the helicopter to take one of the ship's crew up for a joy ride, or as an "observer," as I'm sure it was officially logged. There was a sign-up sheet on the mess deck for whoever wanted a turn. However, most of the crew had a flight quarters billet, so most did not bother to sign up. That left only the "passengers" to sign up for joy rides. The "passengers" of course, were not actual passengers, but the day-workers such as yeomen and storekeepers who earned that title by never having to stand a watch underway. They simply went to the ship's office from eight-to-four, and after that they were done. They could sleep all night, every night, uninterrupted, while the rest of the ship's company, including officers, stood watches around the clock.

All questions asked by the Captain, unless otherwise specifically addressed, were intended for the junior officer currently on watch as the Officer of the Deck. There was a momentary panic as junior officers were programmed to never be unprepared for a question from the Captain. The panic was short-lived, however, as the Captain did not wait for an answer.

"Why don't we let Petty Officer Gilheany go up on this flight; this is his last patrol."

I was shocked to hear the Captain, sitting directly behind me, say this. First of all, I didn't think the Captain had any idea that it was my last patrol, and I certainly didn't think the Captain paid any attention to who was going up in the helicopter for a joy ride.

"Yes, sir, Captain," came the reply from the Officer of the Deck who immediately grabbed the phone and called below to make it happen.

"Someone relieve Petty Officer Gilheany of the helm."

No one asked me, mind you. So I just stayed quiet observing it all, still a little in shock that they were going to hold this flight up for me to go on a joy ride I didn't ask for. But I was flattered. The Captain had never done this before. I knew he quietly appreciated my abilities as a quartermaster and was rewarding me for a job well done. If I could have respectfully declined, I would have been just as happy on my helm watch knowing that he appreciated my hard work, but the Captain of a military ship is not questioned.

My Maine-i-ac buddy relieved me of the helm. I turned to the Captain sitting in his raised chair behind me and said, "Thanks, Captain." I hustled down below to the helicopter hangar. It was strange to see all the hoses and guys in fire-fighting suits. Even though I had been on the *Bear* for three years and had been through many flight quarters, I had never seen anything that went on down below, because I was always steering the ship. I found some guys from the helicopter flight crew and checked in.

Aviators are different from sailors. Officers and enlisted men alike are much less formal and uptight, and are not big on the military bearing stuff. I suppose the reason being that what they do is so dangerous, and their crews are so small, they really have to depend upon each other to survive. It doesn't leave much room for those divisions of rank and privilege. And of course, they are Coast Guard aviators, issued their own sunglasses and leather jackets; they were just too cool for all that.

They gave me a green flight suit and told me I had to go change into it. I remember being heckled a bit by some shipmates as they saw me emerge in the unfamiliar flight gear. At the helicopter, which was tied down to the slightly pitching deck, one of the flight crew gave me a helmet and some survival gear to put on. Our crash teams were squatting in nets hanging over the side of the flight deck with just their helmeted heads visible. The helicopter crewmember told me to get in the left pilot's seat, while the pilot climbed into the pilot's seat to the right of me.

Years after my tour of duty on the Coast Guard Cutter *Bear* was over, I was a bit surprised to see one of the Coast Guard helicopters we used to land on the *Bear* on display at the Smithsonian Air and Space Museum. The helicopters were HH52-A, built by Sikorsky Aircraft Corporation in 1963. These helicopters were big and boxy and were said to have a boat's hull designed to land on the water for rescues. The Coast Guard did not adopt a rescue swimmer program until the 1980's.[22] The HH52-A was the backbone of the Coast Guard aviation program for a generation.

As I sat in the unfamiliar chair and looked around, I found the interior of the helicopter a bit unnerving. The outside looked so nice, painted white with red and blue racing stripes. I assumed the interior would be finished, but it was not. It was bare metal with exposed wires and cables running throughout. The control console in front of us was particularly scary: just an aluminum dashboard with gauges on top while all the wires were exposed and coming out of the bottom. The front of it was curved to fit the shape of the windshield, but when the helicopter engine fired up, it started to vibrate—I realized it wasn't even secured to the windshield. The entire console was supported by a single aluminum stanchion not unlike the removable tables in a custom van.

As I was taking all of this in, one of the flight crew crawled up between the pilot and myself to give me a safety briefing. He

The day I flew a helicopter.

In the co-pilot seat.

didn't even bother to explain the harness system; he just went ahead and locked me in the seat.

"If we crash, grab hold of the bottom of the seat to orientate yourself. After impact the helo will probably fill with water and capsize. Hold your breath. Wait until it stops moving. Then pull this lever to open the door and swim out. If you are disoriented, blow out some bubbles and follow them to the surface. This is your lifejacket," he concluded, pointing to the toggle on the inflatable life preserver.

"Wait, that's it?" I thought as he crawled to his seat in the back of the helo, confident in his ability to save himself, having practiced similar maneuvers in a swimming pool many times before. I would receive this same briefing fifteen years later while flying out to a cutter after 9/11. By then I was an older chief warrant officer, and more confident in my inabilities. I listened politely to the same briefing from the crewman, and then I grabbed his arm, looked him in the eye, and said, "Listen, if we crash, I'm counting on you to save my ass. Got it?" By the look on his face I could tell he hadn't flown too many warrant boatswains before. "Yes, sir," he said with a puzzled look on his face. But now I was only twenty-two years old and I had to believe I could successfully execute such a maneuver based solely on a forty-five-second safety briefing. But then, I was invincible, and I did believe it.

It got very loud immediately after the rotors started to spin above our heads. The pilot was completing his checks and talking to our operations guys in our combat information center below the bridge. A crewman with a colored jersey and crash helmet came running up to the side of the helo to disconnect the tie-downs. I had recorded all of these steps in the ship's log many times before and was now seeing them done for the first time.

It was time to go. The pilot reached down with his left hand and took hold of the collective. It was a big lever near the floor between the seats. His right hand was on the stick and his two feet were on the pedals. Then, as if driving a car, he simply pulled up on the collective and as soon as we were about six feet off the deck, he made the helo bank hard right and took off to starboard. As we continued to climb, I looked back at the ship for as long as I could, having never seen her from those angles before.

"First time in a helo?" I heard the pilot ask me through the intercom system in our helmets.

"Yes, sir."

"Don't call me sir. Up here, I'm Tom."

This might have been the first time I heard such a comment from an officer, but it wouldn't be the last. I found it strange at the time, but it wasn't until later in my career that I realized why. While some enlisted people found this to be an indication of a "cool" officer, I had a different take. "Coolness" was not a trait I looked for in the officers appointed over me. As far as I was concerned, any officer who said, "Don't call me sir" was just trying to have his cake and eat it, too. Besides, you can rest assured we'd all be calling them "sir" when it suited them. But sitting in this helicopter, flying high above the turquoise blue water of the Bahama Islands, I simply replied out of habit, "Yes, sir."

"You see this needle right here?"

"Yes," I responded, trying hard to not say "sir."

"This is the TACAN needle, and it's always pointing to the TACAN antenna on the ship." As we flew away from the ship, the needle was pointing 180 degrees relative, directly behind us, or in the six o'clock position. We would continue to fly away from the ship for an hour in search of "contacts," which is how we referred to vessels of all kinds, and then come about and head back to the ship, having used up our allotted fuel. These helo flights were very important to the Captain of the cutter they were assigned to, as it was their best chance of locating and busting a drug smuggler.

The co-pilot's seat has all the same controls as the pilot's seat, so every time he moved the stick, the co-pilot's stick on my side would move accordingly. I made sure to keep away from all the controls, not wanting to be the cause of our demise and having to execute that escape maneuver. I didn't think it was my place to start asking questions about how to fly the helicopter, but luckily for me the pilot spent the entire first hour of the flight explaining the inner workings of the helicopter in great detail, including all of the controls and gauges in the rickety console in front of us. We hadn't found many contacts worth investigating (which the Captain would not be pleased about), but it did allow plenty of time for my tutorial.

"Stand-by, we're coming about," said the pilot to the entire crew through the helmet intercom. Our hour of fuel was up. The helo started a hard turn to starboard. I instinctively reached for something to grab hold of. I looked past the pilot out his window and all I could see was the sea below. I wondered if they always made such severe turns, or if they just liked messing with ship guys. The helo leveled out after the 180-degree turn and the pilot settled on a course.

"Ok, you got her," he said.

My natural instinct when given any order was to reply, "Yes, sir." However, in this instance my survival instinct prevailed.

"Oh, no thanks, that's OK, thanks . . ."

"Go ahead, you got her. I'm not going to let us crash."

I noticed his hand was no longer on the stick.

I put my right hand on my stick and started to think, "how do I know what direction to steer in? Are we climbing, falling, or maintaining altitude?"

Luckily, the pilot read my mind.

"Remember, this TACAN needle is always pointing to the TACAN antenna on the ship."

"So all I have to do is keep the needle lined up with the lubber's line and we'll get back to the ship?"

"That's right."

The lubber's line is a mark on the fixed part of a compass indicating the twelve o'clock position, or 0-0-0 degrees relative. I noticed the needle was not pointing to the lubber's line, but was pointing about fifteen degrees to port.

"So the ship's over there," I said, pointing off the port bow, "and we need to turn about fifteen degrees to port."

"Correct."

I thought to myself, "OK, here she goes," as I pushed the stick to the left. The helicopter leaned to port as I waited for the needle to move to the right and line up with the twelve o'clock position on the dial. Flying at this altitude, there was nothing to relate to visually. I had to rely on the instruments to see if the helicopter was turning. It wasn't. I pushed the stick harder to port but the needle wouldn't move, even though we were flying sideways with a port list.

"I'm moving the stick, but we're not turning."

"That's because you didn't give it any pedals. The pedals change the pitch of the tail rotor and allow the helicopter to turn."

"Oh, OK," I said as I pressed down on one pedal.

The needle started to move to the right and eventually lined up with the twelve o'clock position. We were on course back to the *Bear*. I continued to make minor course changes using the stick and the pedals, as we continued to search for a good drug smuggler to bust before we got back to the ship empty handed. The pilot eventually started talking to the *Bear* over the radio and turned his attention away from me. It was probably only for a few minutes, but for those few minutes, a guy who was recently swigging quarts of beer and dreaming on a New York City stoop was now flying a Coast Guard helicopter around the Bahamas.

"How am I doing?" I asked anxiously as soon as the pilot got off the radio. He looked at all the gauges and said, "Not bad, except that we're falling about one hundred feet per minute." He reached down and pulled up on the collective, the lever between the seats.

"Every time you make a course adjustment you lose a little torque, so you have to pull up on the collective to compensate."

I was proud of myself, but happy he got off the radio when he did. A few minutes later, the lesson was over.

"I've got the plane."

I didn't know what was stranger, the fact that they called a helicopter a plane, or that in an instant he could change from my buddy Tom to the aircraft commander. Even his tone of voice changed. As the helicopter leaned hard to starboard, we started into what can only be described as a corkscrew dive. Moments later, we were in a hover about seventy-five feet above a Dominican fishing boat. I looked downward at the scared Dominican fishermen, who looked up at us while clinging to the piles of nets under them as their eighty-foot fishing boat, lined with griped-down, rubber dinghies, plowed through the seas. After the description of the vessel and her identifying numbers were relayed back to the *Bear*, we started back up to cruising altitude. The intelligence check must have come back "negative" on the fishing boat.

We had enough fuel for one more diversion. The pilot said, "Let's go check out that one over there," and pointed to what appeared to be a ship off the starboard side, near the south shore of Great Inagua Island. He turned the helo in the direction of the contact and we watched it closely as it eventually became more visually distinct.

"Shit."

The pilot had realized it at the same time as I did. We were intercepting an old wreck of a ship near the beach. We should have checked the chart, which I then looked for instinctively. I found an aeronautical chart stuffed next to the seat. It was close enough to the nautical charts I was used to and I quickly found that our contact was indeed a charted wreck. To make matters worse, by the look of the rusty hulk, it had been there for quite a while. No excuse. Being a quartermaster, I felt somewhat responsible for this boondoggle, but that was silly. Had I allowed an officer on the ship to make the same mistake, I would have been in trouble. We both knew the Captain would fail to see the humor in our having used up our last bit of gas to check out a shipwreck.

We made it back to the ship and landed uneventfully. The pilot made it clear, in his cool aviator way, that this episode would not be discussed on board the ship and that he would handle it. He said nothing else about it. I was impressed by his confidence in my discretion. It was clear that these aviators were loyal to their own crewmembers first and foremost. I suppose that's what putting your life in other guys' hands day after day will earn you. I have no idea what he passed to the ship about that final contact, and I really didn't care. I was grateful for the lesson and happy to keep Tom's secret.

Flying a helicopter was something I had no interest in but turned out to be one of the most memorable experiences of my life. It was one of many unexpected rewards I would earn for my hard work, but the best was still yet to come.

CHAPTER / 7

Tall Ship Sailor

The South Street Seaport Museum is situated on the East River in lower Manhattan just below the Brooklyn Bridge. It was about an hour's ride on the Second Avenue bus from our home on 82nd Street. My mother made sure to get us out of our tiny Yorkville apartment as often as she could. She had a regular assortment of day trips we'd cycle through and embark on via public transportation. This was another spring day in New York City spent at one of my favorite childhood places, a place where I dreamed many dreams.

"Look, the *Eagle* is coming here on the Fourth of July for Operation Sail," my mother told us as she sat on the bench. It was 1976, and she was only forty years old at the time, which seems strange now as I remember her seeming so much older. She was a round Irish woman: the kind who might wear a raincoat on dry days and refused to allow her picture to be taken. She was very Catholic and very protective of the three of us, perhaps to a fault.

My sister and I sat on the bench on one side of her, and my brother sat on the other. I was twelve years old and the youngest. My sister was a year and change older than me, and my brother was a year and change older than her. I was closer to my sister, not just in age, but also in spirit. We played together for countless hours on those museum ships, especially the fishing schooner *Lettie G. Howard*, and the *Ambrose* lightship. My father, who at the time had put together a couple years of sobriety, was preoccupied with recovering from alcoholism and was never involved in our daily life. My brother was always there, but he was a bit disengaged. He remembered what life was like prior to the restraining order, which my young memory mercifully spared me from. If my brother had any dreams of his own, they dwelt elsewhere. My mother believed in the value of dreaming a good dream and shared that gift with us, despite her inability to achieve many of her own dreams during her lifetime. For the most part, she was only able to interact with her dreams in prayer. As for my twelve-year-old self, I dreamed big.

The museum owned two large sailing ships, or tall ships as they are called, for display and tours. There was the *Watertree*, a 325-foot fully rigged ship (a ship with square sails on all masts), and the *Peking*, a 377-foot barque (a ship with square sails on all masts but the last mast). Although I had assembled plastic models of the clipper ship *Cutty Sark* and the whaling ship *Charles W. Morgan* with my trusty tube of Duco Cement, these were the only two real tall ships I had ever seen. My sister and I took the piece of promotional material and looked at the picture of the U.S. Coast Guard Cutter *Eagle* underway under full sail. We had no idea that the Coast Guard had a tall ship, never mind one that actually sailed.

The *Eagle* is a 295-foot, three-masted barque operated as a training vessel by the U.S. Coast Guard Academy in New London, Connecticut. It was originally built in 1936 in Hamburg, Germany as a sail-training vessel for the German navy.[23] Originally called *Horst Wessel*, she was named after a Nazi martyr who penned the Nazi national anthem. Rudolph Hess delivered the remarks

U.S.C.G.C. *Eagle* underway, full sail.

at her commissioning in the presence of the Fuhrer. She was the flagship of the Nazi Navy training fleet.[24] Legend has it that Adolf Hitler may have come on board for a visit on occasion.

The Coast Guard Academy had a long tradition of sail training so at the end of the war, when the Superintendent of the Academy became aware that the *Horst Wessel* was coming available as a war prize, he told one of his commanders, Gordon McGowan, to take a few guys over to Germany and bring it back as the Coast Guard Cutter *Eagle*. Commander McGowan, the first commanding officer of the *Eagle*, flew over to Germany with eight or so other Coast Guardsmen to take possession of the *Horst Wessel*.[25] Both crews, German and American, spent months scrounging around bombed-out Bremerhaven gathering stores and supplies to make the ship ready for sea.[26]

Conveniently, the *Horst Wessel* already had a figurehead on the bow, which was an eagle. This coincidence was due to the eagle being widely used as a Nazi symbol. There was only one major problem with that: the eagle was clutching a swastika. During the months of preparation in Bremerhaven, one of the German *Horst Wessel* officers presented Commander McGowan with a carved piece of teak in the shape of the Coast Guard shield as a gift. The swastika was removed from the figurehead's talons and was replaced with the Coast Guard shield.[27] She was commissioned as the U.S.C.G.C. *Eagle* on May 15, 1946.[28] They made the trip across the Atlantic with a crew made up of approximately two-thirds Coast Guardsmen, and one-third German sailors.[29] Coast Guardsmen have been proudly training on her ever since.

We were excited about the prospect of being able to see the *Eagle* and take a tour, and we all decided that we would have to come back on the Fourth to see her.

July 4, 1976—

The Bicentennial of the United States was finally here. There had been a great deal of anticipation and hype around the events leading up to this day. We were in Battery Park at the southern tip of Manhattan Island to view Operation Sail. It was a parade of tall ships from all over the world, led, of course, by the *Eagle*. It was hard to see anything, given the sea of people engulfing us, and though our square Kodak snapshots (with the white borders) didn't reveal much more when we finally got them back from the developer, we were happy to be there regardless.

When the parade of tall ships passed, we quickly made our way up to South Street Seaport to meet the *Eagle* and take a tour. When we arrived, there was another crowd of people to deal with, but I didn't give that much thought because there she was, the most beautiful ship I had ever seen, already tied up to the pier we had spent so many days playing on. Her glistening white hull bore those signature red and blue Coast Guard racing stripes near the bow—she was easily distinguishable from every other tall ship. Her masts rose 150 feet in the air; she was a sight to see. We got in line to take a tour. After about three hours, we finally made it to the gangway. When we got on board, every inch of the pinrails was covered with lines leading down from the yardarms, all neatly coiled and hanging on the appropriate belaying pin. I thought it was the coolest ship in the world. We made our way back aft to the ship's wheel. It was exciting to get to hold onto the wheel and pretend to steer. I had no idea that the opportunity to sail on a tall ship still existed in this modern age, and I dreamed about what it would be like if I was one day given that opportunity. I decided then that I had to try, and that I ought to join the U.S. Coast Guard.

In January 1986, I was completing my first tour of duty in the Coast Guard and due to be transferred off of the Cutter *Bear* that coming summer. We were required to submit a "dream sheet" to our detailer at Coast Guard Headquarters and list our dream billets. As I enjoyed chasing drug smugglers, I asked for more large Coast Guard cutters stationed out of Florida. My detailer had different ideas. When I finally got him on the phone, he told me he wanted to assign me to the Coast Guard Cutter *Wedge* in New Orleans. I had never heard of the *Wedge*. It was a construction tender, which meant it was a seventy-five-foot towboat with a pile driving crane barge used to build aids to navigation. I was a second-class petty officer, or E-5, at the time. It was independent duty, which meant I would be the only quartermaster on board. Independent duty billets were reserved for top performers, and I was expected to be proud of this assignment.

As I was resigning myself to my new assignment, it occurred to me that I hadn't tried to get on the *Eagle*. The *Eagle* belonged to the Academy and it seemed unlikely that I might be assigned. For some reason though, now the thought came to me for the first time since joining the Coast Guard. I did some research and went to speak to my lieutenant about the possibility. We found out that the *Eagle* sailed from March until September each year and thirty temporary crewmembers are assigned on board annually. As fate would have it, one of those billets was for a second-class quartermaster.

Competition for these assignments was very tight, and a strong command recommendation was required. In order for me to get the billet I would have to depart the *Bear* months early, with no replacement. It seemed like a real longshot. My lieutenant discussed it with the command and soon reported back that they would do whatever they could to get me "temporary duty en route" orders to the *Eagle* and extend my New Orleans reporting date to late September. It wasn't long after that when I received orders to report aboard the U.S. Coast Guard Cutter *Eagle*. I was going to be a tall ship sailor after all.

In March of 1986, I moved everything I owned from my locker and my rack on the *Bear* to the trunk of my 1975 Delta 88 convertible. I saluted the flag flying from the stern of the *Bear* one last time as I walked down the gangway and drove off on my new adventure. After a few days visiting my very proud mother in our tiny Yorkville apartment, I headed up to New London, Connecticut.

I was impressed as I drove onto the grounds of the Coast Guard Academy with the manicured parade field and red brick colonial style buildings. The academy sits on a bluff on the west bank of the Thames River. As I headed down the hill to the waterfront, the *Eagle* eventually came into view. I hadn't seen her in many years; I was just as impressed with her as I was the first time I laid eyes on her. I parked my car, grabbed my sea bag, and I reported aboard in full dress blues, as was required.

I was shown to my rack in the crew berthing up forward. Even the lay-out was based upon tradition. The enlisted crew lived up forward, as that is the roughest riding portion of any ship. The cadets, or midshipmen as the Navy calls their cadets, were housed amidships, and the officers lived back aft in the easiest riding portion of the ship.

I was told that I was assigned to the foremast as my emergency billet during "sail stations." I was used to the standard emergency drills, fire, man overboard, abandon ship, but sail stations was new to me. It was explained that if the ship was under sail and a squall came quickly upon us, the crew would have to scramble up the mast and out onto the yardarms to douse the top two sails, the royal and topgallant. Otherwise, a microburst in a thunderstorm could knock the ship down and sink her. Unfortunately, this actually happened a couple of months later to the topsail schooner *Pride of Baltimore*, on May 14, 1986, during a squall just north of Puerto Rico.[30]

I put on my work uniform and reported to the foremast. The first order of business for anyone reporting aboard was to complete an "up-and-over drill." The first class boatswain's mate in charge of the foremast instructed us to "climb up the starboard side of the mast to the cross tree, and come down the port side." We were expected to do it safely and without delay. On a ship, especially one such as this, everyone must be able to perform in the worst of conditions. If anyone was found to be afraid of heights, or unable to do it for whatever reason, they could not remain on the *Eagle*. There was one other new guy with me as

I recall. We didn't hesitate. We climbed up onto the outer rail in front of the ratlines, the black spider web structures leading down from each section of mast. I focused on where I was going, not where I had been, which just seemed like a good idea. When we reached the tops, the first platform about fifty feet up, I realized the platform was directly above our heads. We had to climb out, leaning back a bit to get up onto the platform. This was the most difficult part of this evolution, but thanks to testosterone and pride, we both heaved ourselves onto the tops without incident, and continued on up to the cross tree. We completed the same maneuver to get up onto the crosstree platform. We were about a hundred feet above the deck. After enjoying the view for a few moments, we descended carefully down the port side. Our test complete, we were officially *Eagle* sailors.

Everyone assigned to the *Eagle* wanted to be there. I felt at home right away. Morale was high amongst the like-minded crew and officers. Whether they were fulfilling their own dreams, or were ordered there unknowingly, all were proud and excited about being tall ship sailors. The crew took great pride in knowing the names of all the lines, yardarms, and stays. There was enough nautical terminology being thrown about to make a regular ship sailor feel like a landlubber.

All of the traditions and arts of the sea were alive and well on the *Eagle*. Every rail and every stanchion was covered with decorative rope designs known to sailors as "fancy work," demonstrating the dedication of those who had sailed her before us. Everyone took pride in knowing the most obscure knots, and the crew attached their own fancy work lanyards to their rigging knives with marlin spikes, which were required to be carried by all.

My ability to navigate with the sextant quickly put me in good standing with this tradition-minded crew. Most quartermasters might have known enough about celestial navigation to

Setting sail on *Eagle*.

answer the questions on the advancement test. However, one can only master the art if they practice it regularly. I loved it and had been breaking out the sextant at every opportunity over the past three years. Soon I was teaching the craft to anyone who wanted to learn, be it seamen, cadets, or radarmen. I even taught some eye-rollers, who were too polite to tell me they were not that interested in the fact that Betelgeuse was Orion's right armpit.

After about a month of preparation for the summer cruising season, we got underway and headed to Yorktown, Virginia, to embark the first contingent of Officer Candidate School and Quartermaster School trainees from the Coast Guard Training Center. It was good to be reunited with my Maine-i-ac quartermaster buddy from the *Bear*, who had recently been assigned as an instructor at the Quartermaster School, when he brought his students aboard.

The entire sailing schedule was designed around the *Eagle* being in some port for some festival or special occasion. Besides being a training ship, she is the Coast Guard's showboat. It was the best of all worlds: to be underway sailing and training all week only to be in port every weekend on liberty, or on duty giving tours. There was always some big party for dignitaries held on the ship. A big white tarp was rigged to provide cover for the entire center portion of the deck known as the "waste." The cooks, all of whom had attended advanced schools, made ice sculptures to accompany their brilliant displays of food. The officers were always in full dress whites for these occasions, and the rest of the crew were instructed to stay below, or go ashore and not come back until the party was over. After all, they couldn't have drunken sailors staggering across the gangway and spilling a drink down the mayor's wife's cocktail dress.

We did a number of both short and long cruises that summer. While I enjoyed my underway time on the *Bear*, being underway on the *Eagle* was another experience altogether. Underway, under full sail, the *Eagle* can make seventeen knots. It's a rare and special experience to be on board a 295-foot ship heeled over twenty degrees and plowing through the seas at seventeen knots, propelled only by the forces of nature, with not a single sound or vibration from an engine below. Experiencing this firsthand in this modern age gives rare insight to man's age-old compulsion, such as that of Melville's Ishmael, to go to sea—an insight that very few are blessed with, and I was very much aware of it.

We visited many ports, including Hamilton, Bermuda; Washington, D.C.; Norfolk, Virginia; New York, New York; Halifax, Nova Scotia; Newport, Rhode Island; Portland, Maine; and Portsmouth, New Hampshire. During our visit to Washington, D.C., we provided the backdrop for the Commandant's Change of Command at Coast Guard Headquarters, and watched through the rigging as Elizabeth Dole, the Secretary of Transportation, swore in Admiral Yost as our new Commandant. A few months later, the new Commandant would make the entire Coast Guard, including me, shave off their beards forever.

My duties on board the *Eagle* included supervising a radar watch consisting of one First Class cadet, a senior at the academy, and two Third Class cadets, who were both sophomores. It was designed to instill leadership qualities in a real-life watch situation. I was to oversee the First Class cadet, who in turn was to oversee the two "Thirds" assigned to him. Enlisted watch supervisors were given score cards and were told we were to evaluate the performance of the First Class cadet during each watch, which would be factored into their grade point average.

I took my responsibilities very seriously, even though I was only one year older than the First Class cadets. I was not only responsible for standing the watch and ensuring accurate and timely information was passed to the conning officer driving the ship, I was also responsible for conducting an accurate evaluation of the cadets' performance. It was a great leadership opportunity, which I enjoyed very much. One of these morning radar watches was particularly memorable.

We were sailing near shore and had many "contacts," or other vessels, on the radar. I plotted a number of contacts while showing the First Class cadet how it was done. We needed to pass the current bearing, range, course, and speed of each radar contact, as well as the bearing, range, and time of its closest point of approach. Every three minutes we would mark the radar screen with yellow grease pencil and recalculate.

"Ok, you got it?" I would ask the First Class cadet as I stepped away from the radar and handed him the yellow grease pencil. He took the grease pencil and said nothing. The two "Thirds" were standing behind us doing nothing.

"Stand by to mark . . . Mark, minute 27," I called out.

The First Class was supposed to mark the blips on the radar every three minutes so we could calculate the information and pass it to the conning officer. He did nothing but lean over the radar screen and stare at it.

"Ok, let me get in here," I would say as I made the marks myself. "You understand we have to get this information to the conning officer; he is depending on us?"

He said nothing and just leaned over the radar screen staring at it.

"Stand by to mark . . . Mark, minute 30."

He did nothing once again.

"Is there something you don't understand?" I asked, trying to figure out what his problem was.

This back and forth went on for most of the morning watch. I made the plots myself one more time and turned it over to the First Class once again. After a few minutes watching the First

Class hover over the radar screen doing nothing, I said, "Listen, we really need to get all these contacts plotted."

Then he spun around to face me and yelled, "Leave me the fuck alone!"

I could not believe what I had just witnessed. I looked at the two nineteen-year-old Thirds, who were also looking on in disbelief.

I had no disciplinary authority over this cadet, so I had to swallow my pride and not respond to his outburst. I couldn't believe this guy was going to be an officer in the Coast Guard the following year. Why had he not been weeded out yet? Had they not been taught you couldn't let your personal problems affect your work when the lives of your shipmates hang in the balance?

This was a training ship and this was a training opportunity I was not going to let pass. I owed it at least to the two unlucky Thirds assigned to him. We were due to be relieved in about a half hour. I let the First Class hover over the radar and do nothing until the watch relief arrived. Soon a smiling, super-squared-away female First Class cadet came bouncing into the radar shack with her two Thirds trailing behind her.

"Hey, how's it going?" she asked.

"Miss Conrad," I said before anyone else could say a word, "We're not ready to be relieved."

Her smiling face turned to a look of puzzlement.

"Please do me a favor and tell the cooks to save us four meals and we'll let you know when we're ready to be relieved."

She hesitated for a moment, looking at her classmate.

"Okay," she said as she and her two Thirds reluctantly left the radar shack.

When they were gone I turned to the three cadets and said, "You don't allow yourself to be relieved and leave a mess like that for your relief," I explained pointing to the radar screen. "None of us are going anywhere until every one of those eighteen contacts are plotted correctly and all the information is passed along to the conning officer. Let's go. Stand by to mark . . ."

Slowly, the infuriated First Class came to life. He knew exactly what to do with the radar contacts. After an hour and a half, when all the contacts were plotted, I called for Miss Conrad to relieve us. We went down below and I gladly ate my cold meal alone knowing that I had done the right thing. There was no further conversation with the First Class. I had no idea if, when his anger passed, he would appreciate the lesson or not. I hoped he would eventually understand my methods. I filled out his grade card as honestly, and as fairly, as my hard-ass saw fit. As far as I was concerned, this was the time to affect the development of the future officers in my Coast Guard.

July 4, 1986

Of all the great port calls that summer, New York City was by far the highlight for me. An Operation Sail event was planned for July 4, 1986, in New York Harbor. The Statue of Liberty, a gift from the people of France to the people of the United States in commemoration of the centennial anniversary of the signing of the Declaration of Independence, was dedicated on October 28, 1876.[31] Operation Sail was meant to commemorate the centennial anniversary of the Statue of Liberty, and of course, the *Eagle* would be leading the parade of tall ships once again.

Tall ships from around the world had been sailing with us from port to port that summer. On July 4, twenty-one tall ships would follow the *Eagle* into New York Harbor, past the Statue of Liberty, up the Hudson River to the George Washington Bridge, and then back down again to their assigned docks. The *Eagle*, once again, was assigned to Pier 17 South Street Seaport.

There were extensive preparations to be made in the days leading up to the event. The weather was perfect with clear skies and temperatures in the sixties.[32] At anchor on the morning of the Fourth, CBS television crews came aboard to hoist a camera to the top of the main mast. Thanks to this camera, my aunt, who was taping the CBS coverage from upstate New York, was able to share a nice shot of me at the helm during the parade. Many dignitaries, both military and civilian, came aboard for the ride. The most attention, however, was paid to Walter Cronkite, who rode with us for the duration of the trip while broadcasting live from the stern of the ship.

One of the trip's invited passengers brought with him one of the original copies of the Declaration of Independence. It was in a rectangular Plexiglas-type case, which was about six inches deep. Someone decided it should be placed in our cramped radar shack during the trip. This was not the best place for it, but that was not for us to say.

Soon we got underway and set all sails. The sails were mostly for show, of course, as we had the diesel engine providing our propulsion. When the parade of tall ships began, we were instructed to keep the dignitaries behind a certain point on the deck even with the helm, so they wouldn't interfere with the operation of the ship. It was a bit awkward asking admirals and high-ranking politicians to "Please step back, sir," but luckily I didn't have to do that for long. Soon it was time for me to relieve the helm.

The helm of the *Eagle* is actually three ship's wheels on a single shaft. There is no power steering. It's all straight gears to turn the massive rudder and requires a lot of manpower when maneuvering slowly in port. The actual turning of the massive wheels was the duty of six cadets, standing on a platform, three

Walter Cronkite broadcasting live from the *Eagle's* stern for the Statue of Liberty Centennial Operation Sail, July 4, 1986.

on each side of the wheels. As the helmsman, my job was to receive helm commands from the conning officer and tell the cadets how many "pegs," left or right, to turn the wheel. I was honored to have the helm watch as we passed the Statue of Liberty on our port side during this momentous occasion.

Governor's Island was directly across the harbor from the Statue on our starboard side. Governor's Island was a large Coast Guard base at the time. There were reviewing stands set up there where President Ronald Reagan and President Francois Mitterrand of France were watching the parade of ships. We had a ceremonial cannon on board and, since we had no gunner's mates, the boatswain's mates were supposed to fire the required twenty-one-gun salute to the President. Unfortunately, due to a malfunction the boatswain's mates blamed on the cannon, President Reagan only received a seventeen-gun salute.

Me as helmsman on the *Eagle* for Operation Sail, July 4, 1986.

We proceeded up the Hudson River. There is no enclosed bridge from which to navigate on the *Eagle*. The watch-standers are always exposed to the weather. During these inland waters piloting situations, the conning officer, responsible for navigation, and the officer of the deck, responsible for everything else, stand watch from on top of the small chart house just forward of the helm. Being a training vessel, both the conning officer and the officer of the deck had cadets assigned to them on watch. On this day, the roof of the chart house was packed. In addition to the four already mentioned, the crowd included the Captain and the New York Harbor pilot along with an assortment of others. The Captain was a tall, ruddy-faced, white-haired, soft-spoken man, just the kind you would want for a captain. The New York Harbor pilot suggested to the conning officer what course to steer at each part of the journey to keep the ship away from all hazards. The conning officer would tell the "cadet conn" helm commands to pass to the helmsman. "Helmsman, left ten degrees rudder, come left to course 0-1-2," ordered the cadet conn.

"Left ten degrees rudder, come left to course 0-1-2, aye sir," I responded from my position in between the compass binnacle and the steering platform.

"Left twenty pegs," I ordered the six cadets behind me on the platform.

"Left twenty pegs, aye," they responded as the three on the port side pulled down on the three massive six-foot diameter wheels while counting the number of pegs that passed through their hands.

"That's well," I yelled as I watched the rudder angle indicator, showing the rudder had reached left ten degrees. Once I noticed the ship's head getting close to the 0-1-2 ordered course, I would have them steady up by ordering, "Right twenty pegs . . ." This was taxing for the cadets turning the massive wheels, but it went on without incident as we proceeded up the Hudson.

Eventually we were relieved of the helm watch and I headed back to the radar shack. At the George Washington Bridge, the ship came about and headed back down the Hudson River, around the tip of Manhattan, and up into the East River on the way to South Street Seaport.

Towards the end of the day, as we were making preparations to moor the ship, the Captain entered the radar shack. There was a crowd of us in there at the time. I was busy plotting radar contacts when I heard him say in his calm captain voice, "Hmm, that's some way to treat that priceless piece of paper . . ." I turned and looked at the Declaration of Independence. It had a Coke, an ashtray, and spit-can sitting on top of it. We had forgotten all about it during all the excitement of the watch that day. I immediately snatched it all off and wiped down the case as fast as I could. The Captain didn't say another word. He knew he didn't have to.

We tied the ship up at Pier 17 South Street Seaport to great fanfare. There was a sea of people once again, with many already in line for tours. When I had last spoken to my mother, I told her I would come find her in the line. As soon as the gangway was put over, I went down the pier, smiling as I passed the fishing schooner *Lettie G. Howard* and the *Ambrose* lightship. I found my mother and father in the line. Their fifties were treating them well. My mother's ruddy face had a great smile when she saw me coming in dress uniform, and with her arms outstretched, she gave me a big hug and a kiss. I was just old enough to enjoy it without being embarrassed. "Kevy-me-laddie," my twelve-years-sober father said, smiling proudly while shaking my hand.

This time there would be no three-hour wait for a tour—I brought them back to the gangway and on board with me for

My proud parents visiting me on the *Eagle* at South Street Seaport, July 4, 1986. It was at the same pier, exactly ten years before where we had taken a tour of the *Eagle* and I was hooked.

the V.I.P. tour, which included spaces down below that were off-limits to the general public. We reminisced about it being ten years later to the day on this same pier since we had waited in that long line for a tour of the *Eagle*. It had also been ten years to the day since I decided as a twelve-year-old boy that my far-fetched dream of being a tall ship sailor was worth pursuing.

CHAPTER / 8

Hooligan Navy

Canal Street next exit.

Finally.

The sun had already set. I had been driving all day but now had my second wind with the excitement of discovering my new city. All other "major" cities I had visited since joining the Coast Guard had been unimpressive to a twenty-two-year-old New Yorker who foolishly thought every "major" city would be like Manhattan. I held out hope that New Orleans would not disappoint and had caught a glimpse of the promising skyline coming over what I would learn was called the "high-rise" bridge. It was late September 1986, and I was on the last leg of my 1,500-mile journey from New London, Connecticut. I made the trip in a few days in my red 1975 Delta 88 convertible. The top was down the entire drive just as it was when I exited I-10 and turned onto Canal Street.

At the bottom of the ramp I turned right and steadied up my boat of a car onto Canal Street heading toward the river. I sailed under the Claiborne overpass, and the lights came into view. The Joy Theater, with its brilliant marquee and the huge neon Canadian Club sign on its roof, the Loews State marquee next to it, and the Saenger marquee across the way lit up the street like a mini Times Square. I knew immediately I was going to like this place. It just felt right. I didn't realize it then, but I had just arrived home.

I cruised slowly down the street, with no roof blocking any of it out, taking in all the sights, sounds, and that distinctive warm, humid New Orleans smell—I couldn't figure why anyone, given a choice, would drive a car with a top on it.

After a short driving tour looking for my hotel, I moored up my vehicle for the night and checked in. A few minutes later I was back out to explore and see what world famous Bourbon Street had to offer to a twenty-two-year-old sailor. It was the lady's legs swinging in and out of the window that captured my attention and maybe a few dollars, too.

Bourbon Street, check.

The next morning I put on my tropical dress blues that included dark blue gabardine pants, a pale blue military-style shirt with epaulettes, shiny shoes, and a dark blue garrison cap. That's the long, flat cloth one with points fore and aft. I never wore the big white, round, visor cap if given the option. I always thought I looked like a dork in it. I attached all of my pins, ribbons, and my nametag, then I checked out. I kept the top up on the car so as not to make an obnoxious entrance.

According to my road map, I had to drive down St. Claude Avenue toward the Industrial Canal to find the Coast Guard base. Soon, I knew I was heading in the right direction as the neighborhood began to deteriorate fast. The Industrial Canal, where the *Wedge* was home-ported, separates the Ninth Ward from the Lower Ninth Ward. It seemed the Coast Guard base was always in the crummy part of town. Even Coast Guard Headquarters was in a crummy section of D.C. Although almost 100 percent of the houses were in terrible condition, I still found them pretty. I located Urquhart Street and headed down the last two blocks, past the dog pound and over the tracks, and arrived at the front gate. The front perimeter of the base was nothing more than an old chain link fence running along the tracks. This base was no-frills to say the least. It was a narrow strip of land between the St. Claude and Claiborne bridges, wedged between the Public Belt Railroad tracks and the Industrial Canal. At the time, I realized none of this. As far as I knew there were a couple hundred acres of buildings and grass beyond that guard shack, as it was at the base in Virginia. I showed the civilian rental-cop gate guard my ID and told him I was reporting aboard the *Wedge*. He said nothing and just pointed to the left. I made a hard left just past his shack and drove the short distance slowly through very tight spaces of old brick buildings, anchor chain fences protecting the few patches of green, through the flood gate and onto a dilapidated wood and concrete wharf. On the way, I passed a few Coast Guard guys in their work uniforms, which were essentially the same dark blue work clothes any mechanic wears, except with combat boots and Coast Guard ball caps. They all looked rough and stared at me as I drove by.

I imagined having to drive a quarter mile to reach the waterfront. Instead I reached it in a quarter block. There were no boats of any kind at the dock. As one third class petty officer walked close by, staring at me in my car, I asked, "Hey, do you know if the *Wedge* is in?"

He hesitated for a second, bending over looking at me through the window. "Hold on, let me check." Then he slowly stood up and turned toward the water, which was only twenty feet away. He lifted his right hand as if to block the sun from his vision and dramatically scanned the horizon. Then he slowly turned back toward me, bent over, and looked at me with a smart-ass grin. "Nope," he said, before walking away. Apparently, I was directly in front of where the *Wedge* tied up. I couldn't appreciate his sense of humor, because I couldn't believe he had the balls to do that to a senior guy in dress uniform who he didn't even know. What kind of a place was this?

I found some answers about the whereabouts of the *Wedge* in the administrative offices. She was down at the mouth of the river near Venice, Louisiana. I was informed that some of the crew would be arriving in a government vehicle to drive me down to meet the *Wedge*. I found a parking spot for my car on the dilapidated wooden part of the wharf, next to the other crew-members' vehicles, and waited.

On August 7, 1789, Congress created the Lighthouse Establishment, a government agency that was given jurisdiction over all lighthouses and other aids to navigation. On July 1, 1939, as part of President Franklin D. Roosevelt's reorganization plan, the organization, then known as the Bureau of Lighthouses, or Lighthouse Service, was transferred into the Treasury Department for consolidation with the Coast Guard.[33] The black-hull aids to navigation fleet of the modern Coast Guard, such as the *Wedge*, continue the missions inherited from the Lighthouse Service.

U.S.C.G.C. *Wedge* (WLIC 75307)

The Coast Guard Cutter *Wedge* was what the Coast Guard calls a construction tender. It was a seventy-five-foot pusher tug, or towboat, with a fifty-eight-foot crane barge attached by facing wires. The hull of both the towboat and barge are painted black, as are all Coast Guard aid-to-navigation vessels. The superstructure, or house, on the *Wedge* was painted white, with a spar (tan) colored stack. The permanently fixed crane on the barge was also painted spar and had a red diesel hammer attached for driving piles. The mission of the *Wedge* was to build lights and day beacons by driving piles in places where buoys are not appropriate. Our area of responsibility included approximately 200 miles of coast from the Atchafalaya River in Louisiana to Gulfport, Mississippi, and approximately 250 miles of the Mississippi River from Baton Rouge to its mouth. My job, as the sole quartermaster on board, was to tell them exactly where to drive the piles, and also to drive the boat. There were only eleven enlisted crewmembers attached to the *Wedge*, and no officers. The officer in charge, or skipper, was a senior chief boatswain's mate (E-8).

"Are you the new quartermaster?"

"Yes, Kevin Gilheany, how're you doin'?" I responded shaking the hand of the duty driver.

"We're over here," he said while leading me to the government minivan with almost half the *Wedge's* crew of eleven already inside.

"We're waiting on Senior Chief," explained the duty driver.

After a few minutes of small talk with my new shipmates, the duty driver said, "Here he comes."

I looked out the windshield to get a look at my new skipper. He was about six feet tall, large frame, close to forty years old, salt and pepper hair almost too long to be within regulation, with a bushy mustache to match. He was wearing baggy Wrangler blue jeans and a black t-shirt with the sleeves cut off.

He had one of those wallets bikers wear with a chrome chain attached to his belt. He had a cigarette hanging out of his mouth and was walking slowly towards the van with his head down.

"He's fucked up," mumbled one of the engineers in the back, implying that Senior Chief was hungover as usual. Everyone else agreed, but said nothing. He was too close.

"Good morning, Senior Chief," said the driver as my new skipper pulled himself into the passenger seat next to him.

"Let's go," Senior Chief replied.

As the van started to roll, Senior Chief said to the driver, "Did you get the quartermaster?"

"Yes, Senior Chief, I'm right here," I replied from the seat behind.

He turned and glanced at me, "Welcome."

He turned back to the driver who had stopped the van, "Let's go, motherfucker, we've got shit to do." Then he slid down in his seat and closed his eyes.

Senior Chief only had to curse out the driver once for falling asleep and running off the road during the two-hour trip to Coast Guard Station Venice. Venice was literally at the end of the road, near the mouth of the Mississippi River. There was almost nothing there but a grocery store, a bar, and lots of shrimp and oil field boats. Unfortunately, it was also one of the *Wedge's* major port calls.

Upon arriving at Station Venice, I found out the *Wedge* wasn't there either. Coast Guard Station Venice had just gotten a brand new state of the art building. The previous Station Venice was an old three-story wooden quarters barge. The *Wedge* had towed the old barge out into the marsh and was in the process of demolishing it. We got on one of Station Venice's boats, which delivered us to the *Wedge*, and spudded down in the marsh. The guys on board had already gotten to work. A big clamshell bucket had been attached to the crane wires just for this operation. I watched as the clamshell took big giant bites out of the old Coast Guard Station and deposited them in a pile on top of the marsh grass. It was a nasty scene. It looked like a junkyard in the middle of the marsh. At the time I assumed it had all been sanctioned and approved, but looking back after a few years on the *Wedge*, I wouldn't be surprised if there was a little of the "just don't tell me what you did with it" to this operation.

We climbed on board the *Wedge*, and I unpacked my sea bag into my locker and my rack. I headed for the bridge to formally report in with the Officer in Charge and his second in command, the Executive Petty Officer.

After lunch I changed into my work uniform, went on deck as part of my familiarization and met the guys.

"You're just in time to watch us break in this new boot seaman."

The new seaman, who had recently reported aboard as well, had not joined the Coast Guard straight out of high school. He was about thirty years old and looked thirty-five. He was a small, funny guy with a 1940's wise-guy face and mannerisms.

"No, you have to get on the ball to hook the wire!"

The seaman was standing in the flat boat the *Wedge* carried, which was positioned under the dangling crane hook. They had removed the clamshell bucket; what was left was an iron "headache" ball slightly bigger than a bowling ball, with a hook underneath it.

"You want me to sit on the ball to do this? What the fuck?"

"Get your ass on there, boot!"

The James Cagney-looking seaman awkwardly climbed up and sat on top of the headache ball, holding onto the wire for dear life.

"OK, you on?"

A rare buoy operation for a construction tender.

"Yeah, but I don't know how I'm supposed to . . . Hey, what are you doing?"

The crane operator started to raise the ball with the seaman on it. He raised it about twenty feet, then boomed over the open part of the water.

"What the fuck are you guys doing?" yelled the poor seaman.

No one said anything. The deck supervisor in charge of this prank gave the crane operator the free-fall signal.

Splash! Down he went, out of sight. He was about five to ten feet under the alligator infested water. They left him down there for about ten seconds and then yanked him up.

He gasped for air as the water poured off him.

"You motherfuckers!"

Splash! Down he went again for another ten seconds.

When he surfaced, he was frantically wiping water from his face with one hand while trying to get in a breath, "I'm going to kill you, you . . ."

Splash! Down for the count again.

It felt like watching Oliver Hardy getting dunked in Toy Land, but with all of the violence and none of the humor. Now I knew what some meant when they referred to the Coast Guard as the Hooligan Navy. This was an entirely different outfit from the one I came from. I wondered what they had in store for me.

Just as New Orleans is like no other city in the U.S., Coast Guard Base New Orleans was like no other Coast Guard base in the U.S. The base was a kind of reform school for some Coast Guard guys in the Eighth District, which covered the south-central area of the United States. Any seaman who was identified as a "problem child," and who was subsequently "fired" by their Boatswain's

Mate Officer in Charge, was sent to the Master at Arms force on the base to await disposition. They would be given prime duty assignments such as "captain of their own cutter," which meant grass cutter, of course, or "colonel of the urinal," which requires no explanation. As a result, the barracks on this base was an animal house full of hooligans.

One morning a rumor spread throughout the base that John Hitchcock was missing. He had not shown up for work and it was already ten a.m. Hitchcock was a thirty-eight-year-old third class machinery technician and a first class alcoholic. He was also a drinking buddy of our senior chief, who had been out with him the night before partying in the Ninth Ward neighborhood where Senior Chief lived. Hitchcock lived in the barracks on base, but he never made it back. People started to worry; after all, New Orleans' Ninth Ward was a very dangerous place in 1986. After a few hours of rumors and searches, a guy who passed by the permanently closed back gate found Hitchcock on his back under the gate, with his leather jacket-clad upper half inside the base and his blue jean-clad lower half outside. It turned out he didn't want to pass the gate guard being as drunk as he was, so he decided to climb under the back gate. He subsequently got stuck and passed out. He got in no trouble for this offense; it was accepted behavior at this place.

It was an industrial base, which meant that about forty feet across the wharf was a row of machine shops housed in an old brick building equipped with a number of garage doors down its façade. The workers were Coast Guard civilians, who were all rough, blue-collar types from the Ninth Ward or Chalmette. There were no females around this bunch, which is probably a blessing. One machinist with a long grey ponytail and Fu Manchu mustache was rumored to have a diamond stud earring in the head of his penis, which he would gladly show to anyone who asked to see it. Two guys from the *Wedge* claimed to have taken him up on his offer and reported the rumor to be true. As for me, not only did I not look at his penis, but for the next three years, I avoided looking at him altogether.

I liked being on the *Wedge* from the start, with its small crew and no officers. Even better, our skipper, or "Senior Chief" as we referred to him, took an immediate liking to me.

"Hey, check out the quartermaster; his uniform looks like he's never worked a day in his life," proclaimed the third class engineer, who wore the grease stains on his uniform as if they were medals of honor. His attempt to get the others to join in was short lived.

"Look here, you fucking rube, this is a real sailor," snapped Senior Chief, who rarely got in the middle of the razzing. "He just came off of the Coast Guard Cutter *Eagle*. Do you even know what that is?"

Senior Chief set the tone with that uncharacteristic interjection during my first week on board the *Wedge*. He made it official shortly thereafter when the executive petty officer (XPO), his second in command, arrived. The XPO was an unfortunate looking first class boatswain's mate with buckteeth and bug eyes. Senior Chief had nicknamed him "Face."

"Look here, everyone on this boat works for you except the quartermaster. The quartermaster works for me and me alone, understand?" I could tell the XPO did not appreciate this order, but he knew better than to raise an eyebrow or delay in his response.

"Aye, aye, Senior Chief; the quartermaster works for you."

Senior Chief was new to the *Wedge* as well, having assumed command only a few months before my arrival. The XPO didn't know what to make of him. An Officer in Charge who came to work every day at ten, hungover, dressed as a biker? He only put on a uniform when we got underway.

"Quartermaster, let's go. I've got a job for you," said Senior Chief as he opened the galley door and headed to the bridge with me following close behind.

"You see all this mahogany?" he said, rubbing the bridge window frames that extended 360 degrees around the small bridge. "I want you to take it all down to bare wood and then come get me when it's done, understand?" Being an apartment dweller from Manhattan I had no idea how to do that.

As a rule, boatswain's mates are extremely proud of the condition of their boats. The first order of business is always to get the boat in ship shape. In fact, that's all this senior chief cared about. I respected his desire to have the best-looking boat on the dock. He had the seamen painting the entire boat and barge, even on weekends, as he sat on the tailgate of his pickup truck, drinking a case of beer and barking orders at them.

"Yes, I understand."

I knew he didn't expect any other response.

After scrubbing the wooden window frames with sandpaper for a day or so, one of the other crewmembers noticed and took mercy on me. He told me of two wonderful inventions. One was called a palm sander, which was much better than doing it by hand. But my quality of life really improved when I was introduced to the belt sander. As always, I strove to be the best wood sander I could be, and soon had every bit of old shellac off of all the window frames, even out of every crack and crevasse.

"Good," said Senior Chief as he inspected my handiwork, his cigarette ash dropping onto my recently swept deck. He then directed me to buy the most expensive marine polyurethane available. He knew exactly the brand he wanted. He had done this before. Following his first five years in the Coast Guard, Senior Chief received his first command as officer in charge of a unit as an E-6, and he had been in command of every Coast Guard unit he was assigned to since.

My exposure to boatswain's mates up until that point had been on big ships where boatswain's mates were usually referred to with the adjective "dumb" as a prefix. They were also known as "deck apes" or "knuckle draggers." Boatswain's mates were in charge of the deck force, the non-rated seamen who chipped and painted the ship. Their skills, while essential to seafaring, were limited to seamanship, deck maintenance, and driving boats. All assumed one became a boatswain's mate because his scores on the Coast Guard entrance exam were too low to qualify him for any other enlisted rating. This wasn't too far from the truth. However, little did we know, the joke was on us. When it came to other parts of the Coast Guard, such as aids to navigation and small boat stations and small cutters, the boatswain's mate was king.

From as early in their career as first class petty officer (E-6), a boatswain's mate could be assigned as an Officer in Charge of a small boat station, an aids-to-navigation team and, in earlier days, a lighthouse. That meant they were in command. No other ratings were offered this honor, only boatswain's mates. As a chief (E-7), senior chief (E-8), or master chief (E-9), boatswain's mates served as Officer in Charge of Coast Guard cutters such as the *Wedge*, Coast Guard tugboats, and eighty-two-foot patrol boats. No other branch of the military puts more command responsibility on their enlisted personnel than the Coast Guard does on its boatswain's mates. As a result of this divine right bestowed upon the boatswain's mate, they were rewarded for their arrogance, daring, and swindling, as long as they got results, which they usually did. Behavior that got others in lots of trouble would earn boatswain's mates praise and medals. Good boatswain's mates were expected to have a certain amount of "swagger." I was not the only one who thought that limiting these leadership opportunities to boatswain's mates was both an injustice and waste of talent. But, the boatswain's mates had a saying in response to that sentiment: "Choose your rate, choose your fate."

My recruiter never explained any of this to me. I decided to do some research and was surprised to find that there were two eighty-two-foot patrol boats in the entire Coast Guard that were billeted for master chief quartermasters. I had no idea why there were only two, but I decided I wanted to be one, even though master chief (E-9) was a long shot and a long way off.

"After you're done with the first coat, come get me, understand?"

I meticulously applied the special polyurethane and brushed out all the bubbles with the care of an artist. I also wanted it to be the best looking bridge on the dock. When I was done, Senior Chief got up from his designated seat in the galley where he spent his mornings smoking cigarettes and drinking coffee.

Rubbing the new polyurethane, Senior Chief said, "Good, now sand it all down and do it again." I didn't question him or raise an eyebrow then, or the six additional times he did the same thing. Finally, when there were seven coats of polyurethane on the mahogany and one could see his reflection in it, he said I was done. It looked great. I was proud and Senior Chief was happy. He never told me to do another thing for the remainder of his time on board—except for the time when the cook got transferred and took his red bean recipe with him.

Senior Chief told me I was now in charge of cooking red beans every Monday. He loved the old cook's red beans, and for some reason he entrusted me to recreate them instead of the new cook. In the military, you must obey all lawful orders.

Of course, once I got over the initial shock, I wanted to make the best red beans ever eaten. I had nothing to go by. My mother's recipe for red beans was to open a can of Del Monte kidney beans, pour off the water, and dump some on our plates. I asked all the local Louisiana boys how their mommas did it. That was a dubious strategy. I learned quickly that boys don't usually pay attention to the cooking part of the meal. It was only after I realized that the bell pepper was holding my recipe back from greatness that it started to get good, very good. After perfecting my recipe over those three years, locals consistently agree they are the best red beans they have ever eaten. Twenty-five years later, the recipe is unchanged and has won first place a number of times at the Algiers Holy Name of Mary Red Bean Cook-Off.

My actual duties in port included keeping the bridge in order, keeping the ship's log, maintaining the navigational charts and publications, and keeping track of the aids to navigation that got knocked down constantly by towboats. Once a number of aids to navigation needed to be rebuilt, we would plan our trip and get underway. On average, we were in port one week and underway the next. It was a great schedule and the easiest "sea time" in the Coast Guard.

Every day I had to walk up to the administration building to get the mail and message traffic. I enjoyed this daily stroll, except for Wednesdays. The SPCA occupied the property outside the gate directly across the tracks, and every Wednesday they would burn all the dogs and cats they had gassed the previous week. The stack for their incinerator was only about thirty feet high and as a result, the thick smoke would drift over the base at nose and mouth level, directly in the path of my mail route. I had to hold my breath and walk fast for about fifty feet to get through it.

Each day when Senior Chief arrived on board at ten a.m., he would expect me to sit with him in the galley, read the paper, and chat. Senior Chief confided in me a great deal during our late morning mess deck chats. I could tell he didn't want me to think of him as an asshole or a creep. Why he cared, I don't know. He was not dumb and was fairly well read as far as I could tell. He admired intelligence and verbally abused the dumb-asses in the crew.

At lunchtime, he would eat first and eat fast. After, he treated us all to a dessert of Marlboro smoke, which made me feel right at home. One engineer made the mistake of expressing his displeasure.

"God, that smoke is nasty," he said while waving his hand in front of his grimacing face.

"Oh yeah, motherfucker?" was the response he got from Senior Chief, who leaned forward and continued to blow the remainder of his cigarette smoke directly into the engineer's face for the duration of the meal.

Each day after lunch, Senior Chief would head up to the Club. The Club was a bar on base, and an essential component to every Coast Guard base at the time. Senior Chief had a designated stool there. Whenever we needed him, we knew where to find him.

In port, the mess deck of the *Wedge* was like a TV sitcom. All day long all kinds of characters kept jumping on board and walking through the mess deck door, including salesmen, or "common peddlers" as Senior Chief referred to them. They were given free reign of the base and sold all sorts of new and improved cleaning agents and degreasers to the engineers and deck force. But mostly they just liked to sit there and drink the coffee and shoot the shit. They were such a regular part of the in-port routine that before we would get underway, Senior Chief, who didn't care for them at all, would call out on the loud-hailer for all to hear, "Make sure the peddler is ashore."

It was not uncommon to see the little Italian man who came driving through the base two or three times a week in his old dry cleaning truck, stop and go to the edge of the wharf to pull up a line and check his crab traps. He had been doing it for years, everyone knew it, and no one messed with his traps or told him he couldn't continue doing it.

There were more than just crabs in the Industrial Canal. On duty nights, some of the guys would put over a fishing line to see what they could pull up. One night an engineer got a hold of something very large. I helped him reel it in. It was horrifying: a four-foot alligator gar, which is a big fish, basically, with an alligator's head. The engineer didn't want to cut his line and he wasn't about to go near those razor teeth to get the hook out. So we decided to put the *Wedge*'s fire axe to good use and lopped off its head. So as not to be wasteful of God's creation, we decided to put the head to good use and left it mounted on the dock piling directly outside the mess deck door for the unsuspecting mid-watch to find. It worked like a charm, scaring the bejesus out of him. After the gar incident, we realized there were more reasons than the name of this waterway not to swim in it. But then sometimes people were sent swimming against their will.

"Over the side!"

"No, please, Matt, stop!"

Splash!

Seaman Dee, a young black guy from Philadelphia, had just been chucked into the canal by the third class engineer and was now treading the inhospitable water. Throwing guys over the side was a regular occurrence on the *Wedge*. It was usually a spontaneous event, but there was one offense for which being thrown over the side was a prescribed punishment.

During my first January in New Orleans, I learned that Mardi Gras season begins on the Epiphany, or the Twelfth Night of Christmas, and that it's a New Orleans tradition that a "king cake" should be shared by friends on that day. The king cake contains a small plastic baby, and whoever gets the baby, or whatever charm they used in olden times, got to be the king or queen of the ball. In modern times, on the *Wedge* anyway, all it meant was that you had to bring the next king cake. Friday was king cake day on the *Wedge*. If anyone got the baby and didn't show up the following Friday with a king cake, they were thrown over the side. This happened fairly regularly, and while I was exempt from the usual tomfoolery due to my position, I knew if I ever forgot a king cake that they would have the excuse they needed to finally toss me over the side.

Due to the threat of having to swim with the alligator gars, we would all take tiny slices until the baby was found, then we would devour the rest, knowing we were safe from the dreaded baby. It's interesting now, to think how we turned this tradition on its head.

"Oh shit! The baby!" I said as I extracted him by his two little plastic feet.

"Don't forget next week, or you know what's gonna happen," said the engineer, the self-appointed tosser, as he cut himself a second piece, six inches long. I knew I couldn't forget.

"Oh no! I forgot!" I panicked as I drove down St. Claude Avenue the following Friday morning on my way to work. I forgot the king cake. What was I going to do? I knew there must be a king cake somewhere around there. I drove slowly scanning every business in this poor, crime-ridden neighborhood.

"There's one!" I thought as I saw a small sign through the burglar bars in the window of a corner store. I pulled over, looked around, and headed for the door. The counter was entirely covered with six-foot-high bulletproof glass. A blurry old black woman was barely visible on the other side.

"Can I have a king cake, please?'

"Four dollars," said the black woman. Then she just stood there, not moving.

I was not familiar with the bulletproof turntable etiquette. I didn't understand that she wasn't going to do anything until I put my money on the turntable and spun it around to her side. I did. She took the money and spun the king cake back to me. Saved!

The truth is, I deserved to be thrown over the side for bringing that king cake to work. I didn't even know they made stale, rye bread flavored king cake!

I qualified as an Officer of the Deck in short order, which meant I could drive the *Wedge* by myself. When I say, "drive," I mean drive. We didn't navigate. We were in the Mississippi River, a canal, or a bayou at all times. We rarely crossed open water like Lake Pontchartrain, or Brenton Sound, and when we did I would put down a fix on the chart for old time's sake. And when I say, "by myself," I mean by myself. On the *Bear*, there were never less than three people on the bridge at any given time. On the *Wedge*, it was just me sitting in the chair, feet up on the console with

Preparing to get the *Wedge* underway.`

my right hand on the stick. Much of the time, after a build was complete, I would drive the boat throughout the night while the guys slept. I enjoyed that responsibility immensely. We would go up and down the Mississippi from Baton Rouge to Southwest

Pass, or through the coastal marshes from Biloxi, Mississippi, to the Atchafalaya. Occasionally, Senior Chief would hang out in the other chair, chat, and enjoy the scenery.

"Can you believe the government gives us this big Tonka toy to play with, and pays us, too?" he would say.

Occasionally, we would have to find a place to stop since we didn't build aids to navigation at night. On each side of the barge were forty-foot spuds standing upright, each about one square foot and made of steel. The spuds could drop down into the mud and anchor us in place. They came in handy. We would find a clearing in the riverbank and ease the raked bow of the barge up to it. Then we would slowly come ahead, pushing the bow of the barge up onto the bank and drop the spuds. A 2x12 served as our make shift gangway. We would all go ashore onto the batture like a bunch of Tom Sawyers and Huck Finns, break out the fishing poles and build a fire. Senior Chief occasionally carried a couple of cases of beer for these events.

I thought about my old crew on the *Bear*, and how they would never believe these stories if I told them, such as when we built a couple of ship anchorage markers on the bank of the Mississippi; it was nearing happy hour somewhere, and Senior Chief needed a drink. We had no beer on board this time. As the guys on deck signaled me that they were ready to go, I slowly backed the *Wedge* out into the river. I turned to the Senior Chief to find out where he wanted us to head next, and I noticed he was studying an unfolded piece of paper he had apparently taken out of his pocket.

"Look here, head up river at a slow bell," he told me.

"Boatswain's mate, lay to the bridge," he called out on the loudhailer.

Up the ladder, which is the nautical term for stairs, came the sound of dragging combat boots. Soon the blonde head of a California surfer boy appeared. This third class boatswain's mate, Baylor, had been on deck all day, and was exhausted. He had on Coast Guard work pants and a white tank top. He looked more like an Olympic gymnast than your average *Wedge* crewmember. His bootlaces were undone as he was getting ready for some well-deserved rest when he was summoned.

"Yes, Senior Chief," he said trying not to sound too bedraggled.

"Look here, take Harriman with you and get the survival vests with the pencil flares out of the small boat. We're gonna drop you off on the bank. Then I need you to get up on top of the levee and start walkin' up river, and when you see a bar, start shootin' off those flares. Got it?"

Baylor, standing on the ladder three steps below and leaning with both arms on the hand rail, started to show a slight grin, the kind that says, "Wait, what? This guy is truly insane." He slowly turned to look at me to see if this was some sort of a prank we had dreamed up together. From the look on my face, he quickly realized Senior Chief was serious.

"Aye, aye, Senior Chief," he said as he headed down below.

"Push in over there," said Senior Chief, pointing to a nondescript spot on the east bank. The batture, the area between the riverbank and the levee, was overgrown with black willow trees and thick underbrush, and was full of just about every type of critter that calls Louisiana home: gators, water moccasins, possums, raccoons, rats, snapping turtles, biting flies, no-see-ums, and mosquitoes, to name a few.

"Ok, that's good," he said as I pushed the raked bow of the barge as far up onto the bank as possible so the two unfortunate crewmen wouldn't have to get wet. Then Senior Chief made them walk the plank.

"Jump, motherfuckers!" came Senior Chief's command over the loudhailer.

It was twilight. Baylor and Harriman jumped and soon disappeared into the wooded darkness.

"Back out into the river and point her north and stem the current."

I positioned the *Wedge* just out of the main channel pointing north. We kept our eyes peeled on the right riverbank for the flares. It got darker and darker. I started to wonder if they made it onto the levee safely, or was one of them currently sucking venom out of the other's leg?

About twenty minutes passed before we saw two flares coming from the levee about a quarter mile above us.

"There! There they are!" said Senior Chief. "I knew it would be there."

As I pushed the throttles forward and headed toward the flares, I asked, "How did you know there was going to be a bar there?"

That's when Senior Chief revealed his secret. Like Captain Ahab taking out his secret chart of whales, he slowly extracted the folded piece of paper he had been studying from his left front shirt pocket.

With a proud grin, Senior Chief dramatically unfolded his prized possession while explaining, "I took two weeks leave before reporting aboard and I drove around our entire area of responsibility and mapped out all the bars along the way." He was very pleased with himself. I could tell he thought this was normal and an extremely clever thing to do. I just smiled and shook my head in disbelief.

"Drop 'em!" I passed over the loudhailer to the seamen below manning the spuds.

We were once again pushed into the bank. The makeshift gangway was put over and the more adventurous crewmembers scouted the path of least resistance to the top of the levee. I stayed on board and on duty. Senior Chief pressured the exhausted crew to come drink with him in the crummy river shack dive until four in the morning. A few hours later they would be out on deck working again. Senior Chief would remain in the rack, as was his divine right and privilege.

I have nothing against alcohol, and might still drink if I could. I had a personal understanding of Senior Chief's problem and never judged him for it, or anyone else for that matter. I knew that I was only one drink away from being right there with him. Of course I didn't appreciate it when his drinking affected the crew's ability to get the work done. But it wasn't just Senior Chief's addiction to alcohol that affected our operations.

Rabbit Island was a spot in the marsh off the Intracoastal Waterway near the Mississippi-Louisiana border. It was a good protected spot to spud down for the night. Since Senior Chief's secret map showed no bars in the area, he had made sure to bring the beer with him. After a night of Senior Chief and the few young guys drinking on the pilings on the barge, the crew was up and ready to go at 0600. The engineers had lit off the engines and we were ready to pick up the spuds and go.

"Go tell Senior Chief we're ready to go," the XPO told me.

I went down the ladder to the deck below and knocked on Senior Chief's cabin door. There was no answer. I knocked again and went in. In accordance with tradition, the Officer in Charge had a nice big cabin all to himself, which was the entire width of the boat. We lived in one berthing area on the main deck with twelve racks and lockers. Senior Chief was dead asleep under the covers. After calling him a number of times, I had to shake him. He finally stirred.

"Senior Chief, the engines are lit off and we're ready to go."

"No," he grumbled, "regular workday."

Regular workday? We were in the middle of the marsh. He obviously said whatever came to mind to make me go away and leave him alone.

"Senior Chief says regular workday," I reported to the XPO and chief engineer back on the bridge.

"Are you shittin' me?" said the chief engineer, leaning his left elbow on the port window frame—people who weren't used to me often had trouble figuring out if I was serious or kidding. The chief engineer, Chief Walker, was an Alabama redneck through and through. He liked to play the part, too, but he was very intelligent and an excellent engineer. He was in his mid-thirties, had blonde hair, and glasses. But his most prominent feature was his large belly, which made one wonder how he passed his annual weigh-in. His eyes were fixed on me. He grinned subtly while slapping his can of Skoal on his left hand.

"You have got to be shittin' me," said the chief, half laughing with disbelief.

"What are we supposed to do out here?" said the frustrated XPO.

"This is the most fucked up thing I have ever seen in my entire career," said the chief.

"Should I tell them to shut down the engines?" I asked, looking down at the crew out on the barge, who were looking up and wondering why we hadn't given the command to pick up the spuds.

The bitching and Senior Chief bashing went on for the next four hours on the bridge as we waited for Senior Chief to sleep it off. The truth is we could have gotten underway with the Senior

Chief in the rack as we had done many times before. There was no prohibition against it. But since he had declared a "regular work-day," we had to stay put. Neither the XPO, nor the chief, dared to go down below and share their thoughts with Senior Chief.

"Okay, let's go," said Senior Chief as he appeared at the top of the ladder. It was near ten a.m. He was rubbing his eyes, his hair still uncombed.

"Light 'em off!" the long anticipated command at last came over the loudhailer.

The XPO said nothing. The chief, still leaning on his left elbow wedged in the corner of the window frame, looked the Senior Chief over with contempt while pushing another pinch of Skoal into his lip, but said nothing.

"Pick 'em up!"

Up came the spuds and I slowly backed the *Wedge* into the channel. The bridge was quiet. The chief and XPO found excuses to lay below. After about twenty minutes, we were just below the entrance to the Pearl River when Senior Chief said, "Hold it! All stop." I pulled the throttles back to all stop and looked over at Senior Chief, assuming he saw something in front of us I hadn't. He was standing up and patting all of his pockets frantically.

"Just stay right here."

"Boatswain's mate, lay to the bridge!" he called out on the loudhailer.

Baylor, the California boatswain's mate, appeared on the bridge wondering what he had done wrong.

"Look here, get Harriman and put the small boat in the water. I need you to go find me some cigarettes and don't come back until you find them, understand?"

Once again the young boatswain's mate paused and started to grow a slight grin. Now he knew Senior Chief was insane. He glanced at me trying to hold back what he really wanted to say but still finding the situation somewhat amusing.

"But, Senior Chief, we're in the middle of nowhere. Where do I go?"

"Figure it out! Now git! Get in that fuckin' small boat and don't come back until you have my cigarettes, understand?"

"Yes, Senior Chief," said the young boatswain's mate. He didn't mind so much the bizarre mission, but was mostly frustrated by the fact that he had no clue of where, in a coastal marsh, he was going to find cigarettes.

Baylor and Harriman put the fourteen-foot flat boat with a twenty-five horsepower engine in the water and took off. All they could see were spartina alternaflora and phragmites australis growing out of the water surrounding them on every side. They headed north and eventually saw the old and rickety Pearl River Highway 90 swing bridge. They tied off the small boat to the bridge pilings and climbed up onto the narrow two-lane roadway. Highway 90 was as desolate then as it was twenty years earlier when the actress Jayne Mansfield lost her life in a tragic car accident just a few miles to the west. After a hike in the sweltering heat, they eventually came across a small store and procured a couple of the coveted red and white boxes. Now, if only someone hadn't "borrowed" the small boat tied off to the bridge? They eventually made it back, and for the moment, Senior Chief was sated.

They say the leader sets the tone, and as you would expect, the skipper was not the only hooligan on the *Wedge*. There was an assortment of marginal Coast Guardsmen amongst the crew.

CHAPTER 9

Shipmates and Scoundrels

"**D**id you check the shit tank?"

"Yep, sure did, Chief."

Harriman was ready to go home. We had just tied up the *Wedge* in her designated spot on the dock at Coast Guard Base New Orleans, having been underway all week. The chief was referring to the sewage holding tank on board, which had to be pumped ashore when it got full. The sewage system on the *Wedge* was Harriman's responsibility.

"Okay, go ahead'n take off, as long's everything's done."

"Thanks, Chief. See ya Monday."

Harriman was carrying his duffle bag and heading toward his car. Since he was the first to get off the boat to go home, once he was out of the chief's view, he turned back toward the rest of the crew who were still working to finish up and signaled obnoxiously by twisting his right fist in the air with his pinky and thumb fully extended. He had a habit of doing that. He thought it looked cool.

I had duty this Friday night with Seaman "Dee," as he liked to be called. The *Wedge* had five in-port duty sections made up of two guys each, one petty officer and one "non-rate" or E-3 and below. That meant we had in-port duty one out of five days, which wasn't bad for Coast Guard standards. Two of us would stay on board all night, taking turns being on watch to make sure the boat didn't catch fire or sink. Dee was a twenty-year-old black guy from Philadelphia who reminded me of a stocky Billy Dee Williams. He was always in a good mood and walked around all day listening to Whodini tapes on his Walkman. I was only a couple of years older than him, and since we were both from northeastern cities, we got along great. We both experienced an initial culture shock that resulted from our sudden immersion with these southern country boys, or "rednecks," as we called them. We had many a laugh together.

Once the rest of the crew went home, Dee and I sat around the mess deck watching TV and eating whatever dinner we could scrounge for ourselves out of the galley. Soon Dee would hit the rack. Being the junior man on duty, he would have the mid-watch from midnight until six in the morning.

The watch was fairly uneventful. I took down the flag at sunset and made a round of the boat and barge every hour to check for fire or flooding. At 11:30 p.m., I was tired and ready to wake up Dee. I started my last round of the night and went out the port side mess deck door. As I walked forward on the outside deck, almost immediately I noticed the sound of running water coming from the head. Dee was the only other guy on board and I was surprised that he had gotten up on his own and into the shower already. As I passed the head window, I noticed that something didn't look right. The window was opened, but was covered by a screen. The light was on in the head, as it always was, but inside there was a cheap curtain blocking my view. Something looked different. It was the lighting. Something looked darker in there.

I continued forward a few more paces until I reached the door to the berthing area and went in. I took a few steps and turned right again into the hallway that ran down the center of the boat. A few steps down the hall and I reached the head. The door was tied open as always. Now I saw why the lighting was different from outside. Dee was not taking a shower.

All doorways on boats have a knife-edge at the bottom of the door to prevent water from moving throughout the boat unimpeded. Thank God for that. The entire head was filled with dark brown sewage and it was about a quarter inch from spilling over the raised threshold. The smell was horrendous. At first I had no idea what was happening, and then I saw the source of the running water sound. It was the urinal. It was cascading over with sewage gushing up from the drain holes at the bottom of the urinal. The deluge created a brown waterfall, which poured out onto the deck.

"Shit!" I ran to the door of the berthing area and yelled, "Dee, get up, quick! It's an emergency!"

I had no idea what was going on and had even less of an idea of how to stop it. We prepare for every emergency and take pride in knowing what to do automatically, but we had never practiced a shit drill. The only thing that came to mind was that the urinal used water, so I ran down to the engine room and shut down the fresh water pump. In hindsight, this was a silly and useless thing to do.

I ran back up to the hall and found Dee standing there half asleep, holding his nose and mouth, staring into the head.

"What are we gonna do?" he said half-panicked and trying not to gag.

"Look, man, this shit is about to come over the knife edge and if it does, the shit is going to be from one end of the boat to the other. We've got to stop it," I said.

"Yeah, but how?"

"I don't know, but for now I need you to go get the fire boots and long rubber gloves and go in there and stop it with your hand."

Dee started to whine, not just because he didn't want to, but because the smell of it was making him physically ill. "Oh, come on, man . . ."

"Go! Now! We don't have much time!"

Dee quickly returned with the boots and gloves.

"Come on, man, can't we just . . . ."

"Get in there right now and stick your hand in the urinal and stop the flow, and that's an order, do you understand!"

Dee was almost crying. He started to slowly wade through the three inches of liquid human waste toward the urinal. The sewage fumes were even worse inside the head.

"Go on, put your hand in there and slow it down until I figure out how to stop it!"

"Oh, man . . . ," Dee said, trying desperately to get a breath of fresh air through his tee shirt by pressing his face awkwardly onto his left shoulder.

"I'm gonna call Harriman and find out what to do."

I went to the mess deck and made the call.

"Hello?"

"Harriman, this is Gilheany on the boat. Listen, a ton of shit is overflowing from the urinal and all over the head. It's about to spill over into the passageway."

"No shit? That's too bad. Okay, um, listen; go down the ladder to the sewage tank. On top there's a stainless steel access plate with seven nuts. The socket wrench is right there next to the access plate. Open it up and take a look inside and let me know how full it is. Call me back."

"Okay, will do."

I ran to the ladder and went down by the sewage tank. It was just as he had described it. I took the socket wrench and put it on the first nut, thinking, "lefty-loosy, righty-tighty." I turned the first bolt a quarter turn to the left. Immediately, I heard a hiss and then saw the high-pressure brown sewage liquid come blasting out of the access plate and cover the entire top of the tank before I could tighten it back up.

I explained the situation to Harriman.

"Wow, yeah, that's too bad, I don't know what to tell ya."

I knew now that he had lied to the chief about checking the level of the tank. I was further outraged when I realized that Harriman had no intention of coming in and helping us.

Back at the head, Dee, looking like he was about to puke, thankfully reported that the flow had stopped. The tank had adequately relieved itself. Luckily, it never did spill over the knife-edge of the doorway. Now all we had to do was figure out what to do with about fifty gallons of raw sewage. I called Senior Chief's house but there was no answer. Then I called the Club and the bartender put him on the phone.

"Senior Chief, this is Gilheany on the boat. The sewage tank overflowed from the urinal and the head is full of sewage."

"No shit? What are you calling me for?"

"The entire head is full of raw sewage."

"Pump it over the side!"

"What?"

"You heard me; pump it over the side."

"Pump it over the side, aye."

"Dee, Senior Chief says we need to pump all this over the side."

Dee went to the engine room and came back with the pneumatic pump. We rigged the discharge hose out the window and over the side. Then we started pumping the fifty gallons of raw sewage directly into the Industrial Canal.

That was the easy part. When the liquid was all pumped off, about one inch of mud remained. Dee went down to the engine room and came back with the engineer's wet/dry vacuum. We took turns vacuuming up the mess, with one relieving the other when he couldn't take the fumes any longer. Our mission, as far as I was concerned, was to get the head spic and span clean before the crew showed up in the morning. We were up all night cleaning and disinfecting with bleach, but you could have eaten off the deck when we were done.

It never occurred to me that pumping raw sewage into the canal was illegal. I mean I knew it wasn't a good thing to do, but I had no idea that it was a violation of Section 312 of the Federal Water Pollution Control Act. I was only given two unlawful orders during my twenty-year career. I was ordered once to drop my pants and hang a moon with the rest of the crew while we posed for an official *Wedge* photo. The group commander had been nagging Senior Chief for it. Then of course I was ordered to pump raw sewage into the waterway. Both of these illegal orders came from the same man.

Nothing happened to Harriman for his lying and negligence, by the way. I guess we did such a good job cleaning it up, some of the horror of it all was lost on the rest of the crew. Our only solace was in the knowledge that we left him a vacuum cleaner full of shit to deal with in the morning. It's true I met some of the least squared away guys in the Coast Guard while on the *Wedge*, but I also met one of the best.

"Whatcha say, cuz?"

"Billy, what's up?" I responded shaking his hand.

"How's she runnin'?"

"Well, I have to add a quart of oil each time I fill up a tank of gas."

Billy's eyes got wide with amazement and a smile started to grow on his face.

"What?" he said with a slight chuckle. "That ain't good."

It was after work and we were standing on the dock where I always parked my big red 1975 Oldsmobile Delta 88 convertible. Billy was the second class machinery technician on the *Wedge*, and one of the nicest guys I ever met. He was short, solid, soft-spoken, and smiling all the time. Even when he voiced his frustrations about others, he did so in a deliberately abbreviated manner, as if he knew he shouldn't. His family were religious people, Baptist types I suppose. Billy was the tempered version, the kind who can coexist with other people both at home and in places like the *Wedge*.

"Check it out," I said as I opened the trunk of my big, red convertible revealing a case of Pennzoil quart bottles. "When I accelerate I look like Courageous Cat coming out of the cave, there's so much smoke."

"Oh, cuz. That ain't right for this beauty of a car. We gotta fix that. You probably ain't got no rings left burnin' all that oil."

Billy grew up taking things apart and putting them back together. The chief engineer on the *Wedge* declared Billy the best mechanic he had ever worked with. He was also one of those guys who couldn't not be doing something. He never stopped working. In fact, even if I try, I can't picture him sitting. He helped people constantly, just because.

"We could get you a new engine and swing it in at my Paw's house over a weekend."

"Really?"

"Yeah, cuz, that ain't no problem at all. That's what we do," he chuckled watching for my reaction. He didn't boast, brag, or blow smoke. He didn't have to.

Billy was a local boy from Ponchatoula, Louisiana, a small town in the piney woods across Lake Pontchartrain from New Orleans. Of course, Billy wasn't from the town; he wasn't even from the piney woods part. His family's property was in the swampy woods along the flood plain of the Tangipahoa River, one of the rivers along the north shore that empties into Lake Pontchartrain.

"How much does a new engine cost?"

"Well, I don't know about a new engine, but what we need is a newly rebuilt one, and that will run you about . . . $1,300."

"And we can take the old one out and put the new one in by ourselves?"

Billy smiled knowingly. "Yeah, man, that ain't no problem. Trust me. And my Maw can make us some of those good ole' cathead biscuits I been tellin' you about."

Of course I trusted him. Billy had that kind of integrity. It never even occurred to me to doubt anything he said, so it was settled. Billy arranged for a rebuilt Oldsmobile 350 V8 engine with his local auto parts guy in Ponchatoula. One Friday afternoon, I followed behind Billy's truck and we left the Ninth Ward. When we got to the auto parts store in Ponchatoula, I wrote the check and the engine was hoisted into Billy's truck bed. We continued out of town down Highway 22, a narrow two-lane highway through tall pine trees. There was an occasional WPA Art Deco-style concrete bridge over a river or bayou that most people wouldn't even notice. It was at one of those bridges where we turned right onto the dirt road that led down to swamp level along the Tangipahoa River. After a few twists and turns on the way down, it flattened out and we came upon a small clearing with a small ranch house. It was Billy's parent's house. He pulled into the driveway and I followed. The back door of the house opened before either of us opened ours.

"How y'all doin'?" said Billy's mom, trying not to focus all her attention on her son who she didn't see as much as she needed to these days. After a brief hug and kiss, Billy said, "Maw, this is Kevin; he's from New York City."

"New York City, well my-oh-my, you sure are far away from home."

I think that was all she ever said to me. She didn't seem like one for idle chitchat. She was in her mid-forties, medium height, medium build, and appropriately dressed for her surroundings.

Soon Billy's dad appeared. He and his wife were of a similar age. He looked a bit taller than Billy, medium build; he wore jeans and a plaid shirt. Not a cotton flannel plaid shirt like the ones we wore up north, but one made from cotton twill that he paired with a ball cap that didn't match. This, by the way, was a uniform of sorts in these parts. Billy must have gotten his fill of uniforms at work, because he just wore a dark t-shirt with his jeans and never wore a ball cap. Come to think of it, that's another reason why I liked him.

I spent that Friday night in Billy's parents' modestly furnished, country-style guest room. In the morning, I was introduced to Steen's Cane Syrup on my pancakes. I wanted to love all things New Orleans and Louisiana, but this cane syrup was just nasty. As with Big Macs, I try it every ten or fifteen years to see if my judgment was rash, but I remain unswayed.

Billy enjoyed my reactions to his childhood stories. He told me that as a boy he would never wear shoes, and that he would go into the swamp by himself on Friday after school and come back on Sunday night for dinner. Sometimes his mother would fuss at him if he got "swamp-rot" on his feet. He showed me a small empty jar on the kitchen table and explained that it was usually filled with "coon-dick toothpicks," which, he explained, were bones salvaged from the penises of raccoons and used as toothpicks. He enjoyed my amazement and was disappointed that there were none left to show me.

We went outside. In the daylight I could see that there were two or three other houses on this wooded acreage. Billy explained that they all belonged to his aunts, uncles, and cousins. He explained how their ancestors had owned a tract of land along the river, which had been divided up amongst family members over the years.

"That's the big house back there. Cousin Jeb's." Billy pointed to a good-sized, A-frame house in the back. "They had to have the biggest one, I guess," Billy smirked and headed for my car hood.

That was all you could get out of him in the way of gossip. I respected him for it, but I wanted to hear more. As we commenced, well, as Billy commenced, tearing out my engine, I tried to make myself useful.

"Pass me the nine-sixteenths, wouldya, cuz?"

I realized that my upbringing in a Manhattan apartment three blocks from the Metropolitan Museum of Art, while unique, was seriously lacking in some aspects. I had some catching up to do. What's a "nine-sixteenths" anyway?

"Whatch y'all doin'?"

"Hey, Uncle Eli. We're fixin' to ease a new engine into this here car's all. How you been?" replied Billy, not raising his head from the task at hand.

Uncle Eli had appeared and was leaning on a tree staring down at the engine, trying to think of something useful to say. He was a good 300 pounds, and he wore light blue coveralls, probably the same ones he used to wear when he worked offshore.

"Where's the new one?"

"Right yonder in my truck."

"Who you got it from, Mr. Troy?"

"Jensen's," Billy replied, knowing what was coming next.

"Jensen's?" said Uncle Eli surprised. "Hey, woman, where you goin'?"

Uncle Eli had spotted his wife's truck creeping out of the communal driveway.

"Hey, Billy, how's it going, baby?" said the woman in the truck next to us, temporarily ignoring her husband.

"Hey, Aunt Sally," replied Billy, lifting his head from the work only briefly enough to be polite.

"I'm goin' down to Wal-Mart to get a few things," she snapped at her husband in a totally different tone.

"Wal-Mart? Ain't you just went there a few days ago?"

"Well, I'm goin' again," said Aunt Sally, waving as she drove off.

"Got to go to that Wal-Mart!" thus began Eli's rant. "All these women 'round here, they can't stay put, got to go to that Wal-Mart! I don't know what's so good down there at that Wal-Mart. Seems like they go down there two or three times a week . . . Where you goin'? Oh, got to go to that Wal-Mart. I don't know what these women did before Wal-Mart, seems like they must-a had nothin' to do. Got to go to that Wal-Mart!"

The neighbors all came by throughout the day to visit Billy and to check out the feller from New-York-City. By late afternoon, the old engine was totally disconnected and ready to be lifted out, right on schedule.

"How you gonna lift it out?" asked Josh, one of Billy's childhood friends.

"With ole' man Coleman's back hoe, just like always."

"Tomorrow's Sund'y."

There was an awkward pause

"Oh, dang, I forgot." said Billy, realizing a flaw to his otherwise flawless plan.

"You know ole' man Coleman says people ain't s'pose to work on Sund'y."

Billy turned to me, "Well, Kevin, I didn't think about this," he said thinking hard to figure a way out of the predicament.

"So the guy won't operate the backhoe on Sunday?" I said, trying to understand.

"No, he wasn't going to operate the backhoe, he's an old timer. We were just going to go borrow it," Billy explained calmly.

"So what's the problem? No one's asking the guy to work on Sunday, right?" I asked.

"No, that's not it. He thinks it's wrong for anyone to work on Sund'y, so he wouldn't want us to be borrowin' his equipment," Billy explained without a hint of judgment.

I found this whole conversation bizarre, but I didn't want to show it and kept my mouth shut. Catholic people don't suffer from this specific type of moral quandary. I knew Billy would figure it out.

"I ain't scared-a the ole' man. He's thinks there ain't no savin' me anyway. I'll go get it in the mornin'." It was Billy's long, blonde-haired, bad-boy childhood friend speaking up now. He knew he was beyond hope in the opinion of many around there, so it was decided that he would go get the backhoe in the morning.

"My cousin Jeb's wife, Annie, is cooking you a special feast tonight on account of you bein' from New York," Billy said while packing up the tools.

"Really? Wow, I didn't know I was such a celebrity," I replied, truly amazed at the hospitality and generosity of these people.

After we packed up the tools we headed inside to wash up for dinner. It was already getting dark by the time Billy, his parents, and I started walking across the property to the big house in the back. We entered into the great room of a nice, modern house decorated with pine-country décor and lots of once-living animals. The room was filled with Billy's extended family, who were all chattering amongst themselves. A very long table was set for dinner (it was probably a series of tables set end on end and covered with tablecloths). Billy and I took our place at the table with about a dozen others. The women were dressed in knit shirts and shorts or jeans and the men mostly had on the same uniform as Billy's father. Everyone was very nice, but it took most of them a while to get the nerve up to start asking me about myself. Some of the bolder ladies eventually did. Cousin Jeb, the owner of the house, had long black hair and a ZZ Top beard, as did one other guy with him. A platter was passed to me with what I would soon find out were deer ribs. They must have been at least fourteen inches long and bowed in a great arc. I took one and put it on my plate.

"Get you some more, cuz, there's plenny more where that came from," said Billy next to me, watching my expression for amusement.

"Please eat up, we got plenny," chimed in the lady of the house at the far end of the table, who surprisingly overheard Billy's comment above all the noise.

I took another huge rib dripping with brown gravy and placed it on my plate alongside corn on the cob and assorted casserole dishes. I was a little apprehensive about the rib, having never eaten venison before. One bite and I was hooked. The meat fell off the bone and was delicious. Everyone was pleased and relieved once I made my declarations of enjoyment.

Knock, knock, knockknockknock!

Someone was banging at the door with extreme urgency. I did not notice the sound of a pack of hound dogs outside barking and howling with great excitement prior to all the knocking.

"Oh, who is that now?" said the aggravated lady of the house as her husband jumped up to get the door. "Tell him to go away; we're trying to have a nice dinner."

"Hush up, woman," said Cousin Jeb, reaching the door with great speed as if he already knew what was going on.

He opened the door to reveal another longhaired guy with a ZZ Top beard.

"She out there, Jeb; come on, get your gun! I just seen her down by the crick! Come on, before they lose the scent!"

"Oh, for cryin' out loud, you ain't gonna . . ." said the disgusted lady of the house.

"Hush up, woman," said Jeb, making his way quickly to the gun cabinet.

"Come on, let's go!" said Jeb to his other ZZ Top look-alike sitting at the dinner table. They both grabbed their guns and headed out to join their excited sentinel and his pack of hounds.

Slam!

"I can't believe those fools! Can you believe this . . . ?" The lady of the house was not pleased.

I must have been sitting there staring at the entire spectacle with my mouth open. Everything about this was so foreign to my past experiences that it felt like I was watching a scene from a movie, except I was in it.

"What's going on?" I asked Billy quietly, without a clue as to what explanation my question would elicit.

Billy wiped his mouth and finished chewing his mouthful and said with a grin, "Oh, they been trying to catch this one coon for months, but she keeps gettin' away . . ." He looked at me with a grin waiting to see my reaction.

"A raccoon?"

"Yeah, she's 'spose to be 'the mother of all raccoons' sposedly," he said looking me in the eye and grinning.

I just looked at Billy, raised my eyebrows and smiled. He laughed.

Then I said, "Hey, pass me some more a them ribs, would ya, cuz?"

"Sho-nuf, cuz."

Billy was a great friend and shipmate. Even though we came from opposite backgrounds, we were totally aligned. Life was good in New Orleans. I was making progress on my list of things I wanted to accomplish, and soon I'd be working on the most important one of all.

CHAPTER 10

Southern Belle

In 1859, Mr. Henry H. Hansell, a merchant whose business it was to supply saddles to the western market, built a mansion on the corner of Seventh and Prytania streets.[34] At the time, this location was part of a newly forming suburb of New Orleans. The property was in the heart of a neighborhood that would become known as the Garden District, and the mansion was a massive two-story, stucco-covered brick structure, with upper and lower galleries across the front of the house. At the time, the architectural trend was moving toward a center hall layout with four main rooms, two on each side of the center hall. This provided more space than the traditional Creole design, and it included space for a large formal dining room.[35]

The Hansell mansion followed the new trend with a massive dining room at the far left side of the hall. It was complete with a fourteen-foot ceiling and an ornate marble mantle. On the right side of the mantle was a knob that served as a bell-pull. These bell-pulls were provided in all of the rooms and each rang a different bell with a different tone in the kitchen so that the servants could know to which room they were being summoned. On either side of the mantle were large French windows that lifted up from the floor high enough for people of the time to walk through to the side gallery without stooping. The side gallery was smaller than the ones covering the entire front of the house, but was two stories tall and made of ornate ironwork.

Although the Hansell family and their servants were long gone, everything else, including the bell-pull, was just as I have described it when I moved into Mr. Hansell's dining room in 1986. It was my first apartment and it provided the perfect backdrop for a perfect romance.

"Hey, man, that chick is checking you out."

"Yeah, right."

"I'm serious, dude, she is seriously checking you out."

"Where?"

"Right over there, that blonde sitting at that table."

I looked over in the direction he gestured to—through the sea of people standing around—hoping for a human connection of varying degrees. The dance music was thumping away; perhaps it was "Rumors" by the Timex Social Club. I found the group of girls he was referring to. The one seated was a stunning blonde, the only one in a place full of big eighties hair who wore a straight, Vidal Sassoon-inspired bob haircut. To me she looked like a model.

The Ocean Club was my favorite place to go dancing with my *Wedge* shipmates, Dee from Philly, and Ron, a local boy from New Orleans. The place was always packed with beautiful girls. The kind I liked. The kind you would see in the cosmetic departments at Lakeside, the nearby mall. We asked many girls to dance, and maybe one in ten would agree, but we had to ask. Dee and Ron didn't like the Ocean Club as much as I did. They preferred our other usual haunts where the girls weren't so "stuck-up," as they put it. I never took being rejected for a dance personally. After all, why should they have to get up and dance just because I asked? Maybe they were in the middle of sharing some great scoop with their girlfriend, or maybe they hadn't had enough to drink yet, or maybe they had a "stomach-ache," as the southern ladies say. But to Dee and Ron, they were all there just to feel empowered when they rejected our offers to dance, which is why I took Ron's comments with a grain of salt.

"You're full of shit," I yelled into his ear and turned my head back to the dance floor.

"No, dude, I am serious this time."

"Yeah, OK."

"Yo Dee, am I right?"

I looked at Dee to see his response, not that I thought there was an ounce of truth in this story, but just to go along with the charade. Dee nodded affirmatively while making wide eyes, as if to say, "It's true."

I looked back at the girl who was sitting on the high chair with her legs crossed talking to her friends. She had on a short, fitted knit skirt and a long sweater with shoulder pads, as was the style then. Even though she was sitting, I could tell she was tall and skinny.

"Y'all are ridiculous," I said turning back once again to watch the dance floor.

That's when Ron threw down the gauntlet, "Yo man, if you don't go ask that girl to dance . . ."

Now it was a matter of saving face. I figured they had picked the most beautiful, unapproachable girl in the place, and were trying to see if I had the nerve to ask her. I knew if I didn't I would never hear the end of it. "OK," I said as I walked away from them and straight toward the girl that was surely going to reject me. Little did I know that when I walked away from them, I would never go dancing with Ron and Dee again.

"Hi, would you like to dance?" I said, ready to turn back and return to my spot.

"OK," she said, and as she tells it, she flung her purse at her girlfriend and jumped out of the chair. That was January 10, 1987, and we have never been apart since.

As we danced I saw she was even more beautiful up close. Her best feature was her slight Mediterranean nose, usually paired with jet-black hair, but it was even more attractive to me in contrast with a blonde bob haircut. We danced and tried to talk over the thumping dance music the rest of the night. At the end of the evening, she agreed to give me her phone number, which I had to write on a bar napkin.

Her name was Stefanie Antonia Francesca DiMaggio, a good Italian/Albanian Catholic girl from Metairie, a suburb of New Orleans. Her former boyfriend, whom she was in love with, had recently broken up with her. Her friends made an unusual move, for them, and dragged her out to the Ocean Club that night to get her out of her funk. She was in her junior year as a Presidential Scholar at Loyola University, where her father was the chairman of the chemistry department. Oh, and yes, she was a part-time fashion and fragrance model at the Lakeside Mall. Despite all of that, once we started talking, I didn't feel like I was out of my league. We seemed to click from the very beginning.

I did not hesitate to arrange our first date. There was no sense in playing the waiting game. The plan was made for me to pick her up at her house in Metairie the following Friday. I followed the directions I was given to the Airline Park section and parked my big red boat of a convertible in front of her house with the top down. I remembered she was beautiful, but I had trouble picturing her face. I was pleasantly reminded when she opened

Courting Stefanie, 1987.

the door with a big smile. I was invited into the foyer and was quickly introduced to her mother, who had been standing directly behind her. Stefanie went off to finish getting ready while I was left to make idle chat with her mother. Her father emerged from the den to say hello and soon it was just he and I standing in the foyer for a while discussing the usual things you might imagine.

About six months after this first date, we were at a sorority party where the girls had created a Jeopardy game. Each girl had to secretly uncover some gossip, or a good scoop on their fellow sorority members for each of the questions. I wasn't paying much attention to the questions, although I did enjoy the chorus of girls doing the Jeopardy theme, "Do-do, do-do, do-do, do . . ." Then I heard this, "Whose mother insisted that her new boyfriend pick her up at her mother's house so that her mother could have her father distract the guy while her mother snuck out the back door and went around to the front of the house and write down the guy's license plate so she could call it in to the Jefferson Parish Sheriff's Department to make sure he wasn't a serial killer?" I thought to myself, "What? That's crazy. Who would do that?" The girls were laughing and shocked at the same time as we all awaited the answer to this bombshell. Then one of them yelled out, "Who is Stefanie DiMaggio?"

"That's correct! Stefanie DiMaggio!"

The place erupted with laughter as other girls looked around in shock with their mouths wide open to see if Stefanie had run off to the bathroom sobbing. She hadn't. In fact, she was completely unfazed. On the other hand, my prideful nature had me thinking it was one of the most despicable acts of deceit and treachery I had ever witnessed. I should have known something was up when I learned that Stefanie lived in Loyola's dorm and not in her mother's house.

Stefanie's mother's assessment of me was as follows: a sailor from New York who probably had a girl in every port. She waged a discreet campaign to dissuade her daughter from getting involved with the high school graduate, the enlisted Coast Guardsman, but it was no use. We fell madly in love.

My mansion apartment provided a very romantic setting for this courtship. The first meal I ever prepared for her was Kraft macaroni and cheese out of a box with tuna salad, which is all I knew how to make. But the setting more than made up for the meal. I dragged my dining room table, a wooden folding card table I bought at D.H. Holmes, out onto the side gallery. I covered it with a tablecloth and a candle. We were all alone in the darkness with the scent of sweet olive and live oak limbs overhead, separated from the Seventh Street sidewalk by some grass and an eight-foot-high brick wall.

We spent every available moment together. We would drive around in the big red convertible with Stefanie sitting beside me in the middle of the long bench seat. My arm was always around her, wondering what I had done to deserve all these blessings. My apartment was also conveniently located only one block from the Mardi Gras parade route on St. Charles Avenue, and we watched many a parade from the corner of Seventh Street. That corner remained our Mardi Gras spot for many years, long after the mansion apartment was just a memory.

About six months into our courtship, I began to write an epic poem I called, "The Proposal." On January 10, 1988, the anniversary of our meeting, I read the thirty-two line poem to Stefanie. When I got to the last two lines I got down on one knee and read:

> By your side always is all I really want to be;
> Stefanie, will you please marry me?

We started to make plans for the future during our engagement and continued courtship, and I began to become aware of my lack of education not in a bad way, but in a good way. I don't just mean academia either, cultural things, too. Like, how come everyone but me knew the words to the tune, "I'm gonna wash that gray right out of my hair," was actually, "I'm gonna wash that man right out of my hair?" Stefanie had super smart, quiz-bowl nerd friends who would come into a Mardi Gras party and proclaim, "I had to park Avogadro's number of blocks away!" I was inspired by Stefanie, her family, and friends to go to night school. Not because of anything they said. I was truly impressed by the fact that Stefanie's father's parents had both graduated from Louisiana State University in the 1920s. My father's father, on the other hand, was the first generation literate. I also felt a little guilty about my drunken youth and felt I had a responsibility to catch up to my classmates who would have been finishing graduate school in 1988. So I enrolled in my first night school class at the University of New Orleans, and I would continue to go to night school every semester for the next ten years.

Miss Betty, Stefanie's mother, knew her daughter was going to be taken away soon by this Coast Guardsman. I don't think she could ever come up with anything to hold against me personally, it was just the idea of it that didn't sit well with her. It was not how it was supposed to happen. She eventually accepted the inevitable. However, she never accepted my old jalopy. She thought her daughter should have all the best things, and certainly a vehicle that was less than thirteen years old to drive across the country in. Because Miss Betty was concerned, so was Stefanie. I kept fixing things on the car like the new engine, a new transmission, a new radiator, a new alternator. The way I saw it, the more I fixed, the newer the car got. So, I made my fiancée a promise. To reassure her, I told her that as soon as

I had to fix something twice, I would get rid of the car and get a new one.

On January 7, 1989, we were married in Holy Name of Jesus Church on St. Charles Avenue. We tried to set the date for our anniversary, but no one gets married on a Tuesday. The Coast Guard issued us a set of orders to Long Island, New York, for that coming summer. I looked forward to shipping Stefanie's car and driving up together in the big red convertible, but things don't always work out as you hope they might.

While my personal life was experiencing major changes during this time, my professional life was also in a state of transition back on the *Wedge*. On July 1, 1988, I had been promoted to E-6, or First Class Petty Officer, and was now the same rank as the Executive Petty Officer, who was the second in command and a friend of mine. We called him "Boats," a common nickname for boatswain's mate. Boats decided that since I was now a first class petty officer like him that I should not have to stand duty anymore. Most of the rest of the petty officers did not appreciate this, as that meant their duty rotation increased and that they would have to stay on the boat every fourth night in port instead of every fifth night.

Boats also decided that I should become the Master at Arms (MAA) on board. The MAA is the guy who is supposed to enforce all the rules and regulations on board. This had never been done before on the *Wedge*.

There is a time in most people's professional career when they are faced with a choice, to remain "one of the guys," or to break away and become a leader. This was my time, and I chose to become a leader. I warned all the guys to make their racks, to stow their gear adrift, or I would have to gather it all up for the lucky bag sale. The importance of making your rack and stowing your gear adrift is an important nautical tradition with practical application. If a ship is sinking and a portable pump suction hose is lowered into a compartment, loose clothes and blankets floating around could clog the strainer and not allow the compartment to be dewatered.

They didn't listen, and I gathered up all their gear adrift and stuffed it into a large plastic bag known as the "lucky bag." On a big Coast Guard cutter, you would not see your stuff again until you tried to buy it back at the next scheduled lucky bag sale. On the *Wedge*, I presented the lucky bag to the executive petty officer and the guys had to go see him and explain themselves in order to get the stuff back. This created a certain amount of animosity, which coupled with the increased duty rotation, ensured I was no longer "one of the guys."

"Hey, man, I got to tell you something." It was one of the other petty officers on the *Wedge*, and he seemed concerned.

"Yeah, what's up?"

He told me that two of the guys on the *Wedge* were smoking pot underway and that he had reported it to the special agents at the Coast Guard Investigative Services. He was feeling nervous and was trying to recruit me into his efforts. I asked him if he had told the skipper, and he said he had not. I didn't agree with how he handled it, and I did not get involved since the investigation was already underway. Shortly thereafter, the agents showed up for interviews, and people were hauled off for mandatory urinalysis. The alleged dope smokers obviously wanted to know who ratted them out. Petty Officer Rat deliberately continued to be best buddies with them, which left me, the resented first class master at arms hard-ass as the prime suspect.

A few weeks before I was to depart from the *Wedge*, I was driving home and turned up Franklin Avenue when I noticed steam coming from under my engine hood. I pulled over and figured out it was the radiator, which I had just had re-cored. I called for the tow truck and had it towed back to the shop that had recently done the work.

"Look, it's been gouged out. Someone musta stuck a screwdriver or something in there and gouged it out."

"No shit . . . ?"

I felt more sad than mad. I didn't want to believe my shipmates would do such a thing. I told the shop owner to go ahead and repair it. I went home to explain it to my new wife—how the car had been vandalized, that it was not normal wear and tear. Then I remembered my promise I made to her, that if I had to fix anything twice I would get rid of the car. I could have pulled a "technicality" and tried to get out of it and she would have let me off the hook, but I felt it was more important to keep my word. I had to sell it and sell it fast as we were being transferred. I found a guy on the *Wedge* willing to buy my pride and joy for $500.00. The thing I poured every dollar I'd earned in sobriety into, was now gone.

While this may seem like a terribly sad ending to an otherwise happy tale, let me assure you, it was not. While I loved that car a great deal, I had made a decision during my teenage years to live my life according to principles. Back then it was a survival mechanism; deciding when to fight or not was the usual choice. But that evolved into a process where, when faced with a decision, I simply put the situation in the context of my principles and I would arrive at the correct decision. Sometimes I don't like the decision, but I know it is the right one. So went the car.

To this day I have never told anyone who the real rat was.

A few weeks later, we drove off to Long Island in a brand new Oldsmobile Cutlass four-door sedan with my integrity intact, my mind at peace, and my heart filled with gratitude for God's gift sitting next to me.

For our twenty-fifth wedding anniversary, Stefanie bought my replacement convertible, which I love even more than the original. It was a toffee brown 2013 VW bug convertible. Driving it at fifty years of age has turned some heads, and it got back to me that one of Stefanie's friend's commented that it was the strangest choice for a mid-life crisis car she had ever seen. Perhaps, but we'd rather think of it as a mid-life celebration car.

A framed picture of the big red convertible hangs in our stairway now—a perfect reminder of a perfect romance.

CHAPTER / 11

Hazardous Bars

They say that if you marry a girl from New Orleans, New Orleans is where you will end up living. This is true, but I was allowed to take my bride away for four years with the understanding that I would bring her right back. In the Coast Guard, people are assigned to billets based upon their rate and rank. When leaving the *Wedge*, I was offered my choice of thirteen first class quartermaster billets to choose from. We decided to accept orders to Coast Guard Group Moriches located in East Moriches, New York, which is on the south shore of Long Island about halfway between New York City and the eastern tip of the 118-mile-long island. My family was still living in Manhattan, so we would be able to see them occasionally, which was as much as either of us needed to. A selling point for my movie buff wife was that the Coast Guard housing we were being assigned to was located in Westhampton, just on the other side of the tracks from the Village of Westhampton Beach. Who could refuse living in the Hamptons for free for four years? It turned out to be the perfect place for us to be newlyweds.

The Coast Guard in the Northeast was a little different than in the Gulf of Mexico, mostly due to history. There was a great deal of commerce on the East Coast during the American colonial period, and that trend continued into the nineteenth century. Much of that commerce was conducted by sailing ships and as a result, there were quite a few shipwrecks along the coast. A system of life-saving stations was established that began along the Massachusetts coast and consisted of boathouses on the beach manned by volunteers. The heroic life-saving station crews would row out to stranded ships and bring the people back to shore safely. On June 18, 1878, a bill was signed into law that organized this system of life-saving stations into a new government agency known as the U.S. Life-Saving Service.[36] Another law, signed by Woodrow Wilson on January 28, 1915, merged the U.S. Life-Saving Service with the United States Revenue-Cutter Service, and established the U.S. Coast Guard in these agencies' stead. The Life-Saving Stations then became Coast Guard Stations.

One such life-saving station was built at Moriches as early as 1849.[37] The building I was assigned to work in was a classic pre-World War II Coast Guard station, located on an isolated spit of land projecting into Moriches Bay. It was a large, white wooden structure with a wrap-around porch, a red roof, and a cupola projecting high above to provide a great vantage point for watch-standers in the years when visual watch was as important as radio watch. But this was 1989, and the operations center and adjacent radio room were now located on the second floor facing Moriches Bay and the barrier beach separating the bay from the Atlantic Ocean. The cupola had been relegated to an interesting place to bring visitors on tours and a convenient place for senior reservists to hang out and drink coffee during their reserve drill weekend.

My new billet was to be one of four operation center controllers. We stood a twenty-four hour watch where we were responsible for the proper execution of all Coast Guard missions along the 118-mile coast of Long Island. Those missions included search

U.S. Coast Guard Group Moriches on Long Island

and rescue, law enforcement, and marine environmental protection, and they required the oversight of four other Coast Guard stations along the south shore of Long Island between New York City and Montauk. We were the search and rescue mission coordinators. We dispatched Coast Guard vessels and helicopters, assigned search areas, and performed mathematical calculations on the probability of detecting survivors as well as on the survivability of individuals given environmental conditions. When we failed to locate survivors, we also made recommendations to the district office on when to permanently "suspend" searches.

My lieutenant, a native Long Islander, admitted to being relieved when he found out I was from New York and not south of the Mason-Dixon Line. He had had some bad experiences with southern boys and thought all were inherently dumb. The qualification process to stand the watch was not an easy one, but I qualified quickly nonetheless.

We had an excellent bunch of guys at Group Moriches. Morale was high, as it was a great place to live and work. The summer time was busiest as it was the height of boating season. The winters were long and cold and the search and rescue cases were fewer, but usually more severe—I liked to take good care of the boat crews.

One Christmas Eve when I had duty, there was one radio-man and four boat crew on duty with me. Everyone else was at home with their families. I decided to make my acclaimed red beans and rice with the recipe I had developed on the *Wedge*. We could have eaten in the kitchen, but that would have left out the radioman, who couldn't leave the radios. We dragged the kitchen table and chairs down the hall and set them up in the operations center next to the radio room. We said grace while thinking of our families back home. The beans turned out great, and the six of us enjoyed them together to the sounds of my Londonderry Boys Choir tape; the cold wind whistled through the old windows, and the radios crackled in the adjacent room. It made for a most memorable Christmas Eve, and we made it through the meal with no Maydays.

We had a few boats at the station, but none that were surf-capable, because Moriches Inlet had been officially "closed to navigation," a government term meaning it was not maintained with dredging or aids to navigation. So you transit it at your own risk, which people did on a regular basis. The inlet was quite treacherous when conditions were right, and huge surf was not uncommon. It was so treacherous that the Coast Guard decided to bring a self-righting surfboat to Moriches once for a training class, but when instructors got to the inlet and saw how bad it was they cancelled the training. One day when the inlet was particularly bad, we received one of those radio transmissions we dreaded.

"Coast Guard Moriches, this is the *Lori G*. We're getting ready to transit the inlet. I have two P-O-B. Can you take my radio guard?"

I overheard the transmission from the recreational boat and hurried over to the telescope standing on a tripod by the window. We kept it trained on the inlet at all times. All I could see was a solid white line of surf across the entire inlet. The recreational boater was one of the locals who knew how to read the inlet as good as anyone, not a weekender from the city. He was telling us he had two people on board and asking us to keep radio communications. If he didn't answer when we called, we would know something had gone wrong.

In response to his request, the radioman gave the standard broadcast about how the inlet was closed to navigation. The policy was we couldn't pass any navigational information so as not to encourage people to try it, but we took their radio guard and hoped for the best.

"I hope he makes it. It's pretty bad today. Make sure you have him a five minute comms-sched," I told the radioman, to make sure we called him every five minutes.

Five minutes passed and I still struggled to see anything that looked like a boat through the telescope.

"*Lori G, Lori G*, Coast Guard Group Moriches, over . . . *Lori G, Lori G*, this is Coast Guard Group Moriches, over . . . *Lori G*, this is Coast Guard Group Moriches Channel 21, how copy over?"

"I lost comms, he won't answer!" the radioman said, now standing in the doorway between our rooms looking for direction.

"Shit! Hit the SAR alarm."

The SAR alarm was loud throughout the entire property and never failed to get all of our hearts beating a little faster. I knew the boat crew was running to the twenty-one foot orange rigid hull inflatable boat. We would tell them what was going on over the radio once they were underway.

"Boston, Brooklyn, Group Moriches on the SAR-Tel."

I had immediately picked up the red phone on the wall that was an open phone line between all Coast Guard operations centers in the Northeast. This was how we requested helicopter launch from Coast Guard Air Station Brooklyn and informed the District Rescue Coordination Center at the same time. It would be through this SAR-Tel on October 30, 1991, when I would listen to our Air National Guard neighbors ditch their helicopter in sixty-foot seas during the "Perfect Storm."

"We need a launch. We have a possible capsized boat in Moriches Inlet."

"Group Moriches, Coast Guard 21453 underway. Three P-O-B, whatcha got, over?"

Our boat was underway in less than three minutes, instinctively speeding toward the inlet. The radioman passed what information that we had. The coxswain of the boat was a second class boatswain's mate and the supervisor of the boat detachment. We were all aware that according to Coast Guard specifications, the boat was rated for zero foot surf. Regardless of that, we knew the boat handled pretty well in small surf if the operator knew what he was doing. He kept speeding toward the inlet.

The conditions were so erratic when the boat arrived at the inlet in between the two rock jetties leading out to sea, it was like trying to drive a boat in a washing machine. Ahead, toward the outer end of the jetties, a giant wall of breaking surf waited.

"Group Moriches, we have the capsized boat in sight, with two people holding onto the hull. Conditions are very bad. I don't know if we can get to them, but we're gonna try, over."

"21453, Group Moriches, roger. Standing by, over."

The capsized boat was right inside the surf line and quickly drifting to the rock jetty on the east side of the inlet. The two people clinging to the hull would soon be smashed to death on the rocks.

Surf must be taken head-on. If a boat is caught broadside to a breaking wave, it will capsize. The coxswain made his approach carefully, making sure to meet each breaking wave head-on, and making progress toward the capsized hull in between waves. There wasn't much time in between each breaker to make a good pass on the capsized hull. After a few unsuccessful attempts, with the crew hanging on for dear life with each massive breaker, the coxswain realized it was time for one last unconventional effort.

"Listen up! After the next one I'm going to run the boat right up on top of that capsized hull, right in between those two guys. Then each of you is gonna grab one and yank him onto this boat with all your might, got it? This is our last chance. Hold on!"

They met the next massive breaker head-on, and as soon as they started down the backside of the wave, the coxswain turned to port and pushed the throttles ahead. He ran the front of the boat right on top of the capsized hull, right in between the two survivors, and came to a stop.

"Let's go! Hurry up!" the coxswain yelled, looking at the next wall of water coming fast to capsize them as well.

The seamen on either side of the boat each grabbed their guy and yanked them over the round orange inflatable side and into the boat. The coxswain threw the throttles in reverse, backed off the capsized hull, and spun the boat around just in time to meet the next breaker head-on.

"Group Moriches, 21453, we have the two survivors on board, returning to base at this time, over."

I sent the helicopter back to Brooklyn and called for the ambulance. The survivors were extremely grateful for being rescued, knowing that the crew risked their lives to save them. Had things gone differently and the Coast Guard boat been capsized, the coxswain could have been court-martialled for taking that boat into those conditions. Instead, I drafted his citation for the Coast Guard Medal for Heroism.

This demonstrates why boatswain's mates get away with the shenanigans they do: they are extremely valuable to the organization, and they know it. A few years after this brilliant rescue, I had a run-in with this same coxswain. He wasn't a very nice guy and wasn't well liked. He would send the boat underway for a patrol or training and would fail to tell us. We were required to keep their radio guard in case they had a problem. One day the radioman came to the doorway to tell me the boat was underway again without telling us, or passing their radio guard. This had happened many times before so I told the radioman to just tell them to return to base. I figured if they had to come all the way back, they might remember next time. A few minutes later, the same second class boatswain's mate detachment supervisor came storming into the operations center.

"Kevin, did you tell the boat to return to base?"

"Yes."

"Why?"

"No particular reason other than . . ."

"Fuck you, Kevin! Alright . . ." he yelled and stormed out, before I could finish telling him why.

The senior chief quartermaster was standing there watching this event. He said to me, "Well, Kevin, are you going to let a junior person get away with that?"

I explained that while I didn't appreciate it, I knew that if I pursued disciplinary action nothing would come of it. I had already figured out and accepted that the Coast Guard had a separate, unwritten set of rules for boatswain's mates. The senior chief was adamant about addressing the outrage and told me to place the boatswain's mate on report, which I did. Following a lengthy investigation, the guy doing the investigation recommended the charge be dismissed, because I had antagonized the boatswain's mate by saying, "No particular reason," and besides, they said, he had had a few drinks at lunch! Drinking on duty was not authorized, by the way. The charge was dismissed.

Life was good on Long Island. We were newlyweds, off by ourselves, enjoying a peaceful life. My wife had a job at a local newspaper. We didn't have much money, but just enough for dinner and a show every Friday night. What we didn't have in money, we made up for in free time. We had time to do frivolous things like pick apples at a "pick your own" orchard and make apple pies from scratch, including the crust. I stood a twenty-four hour watch and was off for the next seventy-two hours. This allowed me a great deal of time to go to school and study. I earned an Associate Degree and was working on a Baccalaureate Degree from the University of the State of New York.

My lieutenant was impressed with my work and sat down to ask me why I hadn't yet applied for Officer Candidate School (OCS). I told him about my goal of getting command of my own patrol boat and that I thought my best chance of that happening was as a master chief quartermaster. Some of the patrol boats were billeted for officers, but those went to high performing second tour officers who were mostly Academy graduates. The lieutenant was convinced I should not limit myself and that I should apply. He wrote me a letter of recommendation that sounded so sincere, I felt obligated to try:

From the moment PO Gilheany stepped aboard the Group, he never ceased to impress me with his motivation and abilities. As a Group OOD, he was a quick and eager learner who certified in a short time while quickly surpassing others in key performance measures for the watch position. Although the youngest of any of the nine OOD's I had supervised during my tour, PO Gilheany was without peer in terms of performance and judgment. He consistently displayed initiative in taking care of the many things others must be asked to do, and maintains a continual focus on getting things done the right way the first time.

In working with others in the Coast Guard, you run across a few individuals every now and then who have such exceptional abilities, potential and desire that you realize they are working at a level clearly below that potential. I have always felt that PO Gilheany is one of those people."

Wow! I knew these letters came in canned formats, but if he felt half as strongly as the letter sounded, I was selling myself short. I try to never pass on an opportunity when one is presented to me, so I made the decision that I was going to apply to OCS, even though that meant going back for another round of boot camp.

I took and got a qualifying score on the Officer Aptitude Rating (OAR) Exam. That test is not easy, by the way. It's a lot of word problems like, "One train leaves the station at this time, traveling at this speed, and the second train leaves the station at this time, traveling at this speed. What time will the second train overtake the first . . ." and so on and so forth.

I decided to look up the physical requirements for OCS to make sure I could do all the required push-ups, sit-ups, running, and swimming. Luckily I had been forcing myself to go to the gym two or three times a week for the past year and was in the best shape of my life, which isn't saying much. After doing the physical tests, I determined I was good to go. All I had left to check was the running. I had hated running ever since Brother Veracruz made me join cross-country during my freshman year at Power Memorial Academy when I was really just trying to join the field team to throw the shot put like my brother.

Low-top, white Converse All Stars were a staple of the New York street hooligan uniform I had yet to outgrow. It never occurred to me that a thiry-year-old, 220-pound man should not go running in them, but I did. I went down to Dune Road and measured one and a half miles with my car. I finished the run with no problems and plenty of time to spare. That was it. I was going to OCS and become a Coast Guard Officer.

I went home and discussed with Stefanie that the plan was on, full steam ahead. The next day when I got out of bed, I could barely walk. My knees wouldn't bend. I went to work and climbed the stairs like Frankenstein. I was scared. I had no idea what had happened. It got better slowly and finally went away totally in three weeks, but during those three weeks I did a lot of research and self-diagnosed myself with Iliotibial Band Syndrome. The books I was reading were for running fanatics and they said, although the condition was chronic, you could keep running as long as you injected your knees with corticosteroid.

I went to see our hospital corpsman. My knees were better by then, but I explained what had happened. He said he could send me to see a doctor at the Coast Guard base on Governor's Island, but that I might be opening a can of worms I might regret. I agreed. I decided to see if the manual explained what would happen if I went to OCS anyway. I remembered my chief on the *Bear*, and how he taught us to always look stuff up for yourself if you want the right answer. I was shocked at what I found. The manual said that any candidate found to not qualify for commissioning would be sent back to his unit at the previous rate and rank, which meant if anyone failed out they would return to being an enlisted guy. But it went on to say that any candidate who was found not physically qualified for commissioning would be discharged from the service! That was it. The deal was off. I could not risk going to OCS and getting crippled up after a run only to get discharged.

"Sorry, sir, change of plans. I can't go to OCS after all." I knew the lieutenant would be disappointed when I told him. He looked up from behind his desk and said, "Why? What happened?"

I explained the story about my knees and what I had found in the manual about candidates not being physically qualified for commissioning being discharged from the service.

"That's a bunch of bull. They're not gonna discharge you. They have to say stuff like that."

"Well, that's what the manual says and I'm not willing to risk my career over it."

"I think you're making a mistake. I really don't think that would happen. Do you want me to call them? I'll call them right now."

"Okay," I said, getting comfortable in his chair, looking forward to observing this exchange.

He called a senior staffer at OCS, a lieutenant commander I believe.

"Yes, ma'am, thanks for taking my call. I have a QM1 here with me who is considering OCS and he thinks . . ." the lieutenant went on to explain the entire story.

While listening to the response, the lieutenant's eyes got wide, and an uncomfortable grin started to grow on his face.

"Really? Is that right? I had no idea. I'll make sure to let him know. Thanks, ma'am."

He hung up the phone and leaned back in his chair with a smile of amazement.

"She said that's exactly what would happen. They would discharge you from the service. She said the reason is that you are required to meet those requirements as an enlisted person, too. But if you go to OCS and put yourself in the spotlight and they find there is a problem, they have to discharge you. Good call."

It says something about my personality that I wanted to be right about our little disagreement more than I wanted to go to OCS. I was happy to have been correct about the research that I did and that I had dodged a big bullet. It turns out that joining the ranks of regular officers was not part of God's plan for me, and I was totally okay with that. I had the peace of mind knowing I had pursued the opportunity as far as I could.

It was back to preparing for the Officer in Charge Review Board to get command of a patrol boat as a senior enlisted person. Even though I wasn't a boatswain's mate, I knew I would do well in a command position if given the chance. Making master chief (E-9) would be hard, but getting one of those two boats would be even harder. Regardless, I reaffirmed my goal and started studying hard for the Officer in Charge Review Board, which I would have to pass in order to become certified for command afloat.

I was always impressed by the dedication of our boat crews. No matter how many times we called them out, or what we sent them out for, they gave the mission their fullest effort. Many times we saved people's lives, sometimes we couldn't, and sometimes things turned out to not be what they appeared. One case remains a mystery to me to this day.

"Mayday, Mayday, Mayday, this is the fishing vessel *Miss Gina*. We have a man overboard. Come in, Coast Guard."

"Vessel calling Coast Guard, this is Coast Guard Group Moriches. What's your position, captain?"

"Coast Guard, we have a man overboard. We are currently four miles south of Moriches Inlet, how copy over."

It was about 11:00 p.m., and I had not yet hit the rack. I had heard the Mayday and was already in the doorway of the radio room.

"Hit the SAR alarm," I told the radioman, who already had his finger on the switch awaiting my permission.

I called for a helicopter launch while the radioman took down the latitude and longitude of the man overboard.

"He was working on deck and the snatch block swung around and caught him in the head and knocked him over the side, over," the captain reported.

"Group Moriches, CG27089, underway, 3 POB, over." The boat was underway in minutes, which is impressive, since the guys were already asleep in the rack. One guy was still pulling on his pants as the boat sped away from the dock. We passed the position of the fishing vessel in our twenty-seven footer. The weather was flat-ass-calm.

The radioman tried to gather more information from the captain.

"We lost track of him. We're searching with our spotlight now. He just fell in right before I called Mayday, over."

As our twenty-seven footer approached, the captain of the fishing vessel reported, "Coast Guard, I see your boat's lights coming now, over."

A few minutes later the captain reported, "Coast Guard, we've spotted the man overboard with our spotlight. We're going to pull him up on deck, over."

The twenty-seven footer came alongside the fishing vessel and the crew scrambled on board. The crew of the fishing vessel was standing in a circle around the man who had fallen overboard.

The helicopter from Air Station Brooklyn was now hovering overhead. Before a Medevac is conducted, we consult the duty flight surgeon.

"Group Moriches, Coast Guard 27089, we're on scene with the man. We have no breathing, no pulse. We are commencing CPR, over."

I called the flight surgeon and explained the situation. He explained that even though the helicopter would get the man to the hospital faster, since CPR had been started, crunching the man into the helicopter hoist basket would undo any good the CPR might have done. The decision was made to release the helo and Medevac by boat.

"Coast Guard 27089, put the man on a backboard and Medevac by boat, over."

The boat crew put the man on a backboard and carefully lowered him onto the twenty-seven foot boat. They sped back toward the inlet continuing CPR the entire way; at one point, the victim regurgitated into the mouth of the crewmember administering CPR.

I was on the dock waiting with the ambulance when they arrived. The victim was a big man with a large belly. He was white as a ghost, and had blood on his head and face. We loaded him into the ambulance and it sped off to the hospital. After we wound down and discussed the details of the mission, the boat crew got cleaned up and we all hit the rack. It was just after midnight.

Approximately one hour later I received a phone call.

"This is the Suffolk County Coroner's Office. Who's in charge over there?"

"I am right now. What can I help you with?"

"When did you bring this guy in?"

I grabbed the chronological log we kept and replied, "We got the call at 2300 when they said the guy fell in and called Mayday. We got on scene at 2319 and had him back at the dock at 2345."

He barked back, "That can't be right! This guy's been dead for at least six hours!"

Based upon that evidence, it's reasonable to assume that the fisherman had lied to us, and let my guys do mouth-to-mouth on a dead body. A dead body that subsequently threw up in a boat crewman's mouth. I don't suppose it occurred to the boat crew that someone would do such a thing. I'm not even sure it would have made a difference if they suspected it. They were trained and dedicated to doing a job, saving lives, even if it meant putting themselves in harm's way. Thankfully, the boat crewmember did not get sick or suffer any other ill effects.

I still don't know if it was an accidental death, or if it involved foul play. We notified the Coast Guard Marine Safety Office responsible for conducting investigations. The county and the FBI would also have jurisdiction and hopefully justice was served. Although it was rare, that was not our only run-in with potential criminals at Moriches.

CHAPTER 12

Life and Death Decisions

For the most part, the Coast Guard is revered by the general public, who see them as their heroic rescuers should they ever fall into peril at sea. But the Coast Guard is also a law enforcement agency and is resented by many who have had their boats torn apart by the Coast Guard looking for drugs and other contraband. Sometimes both of these points of view can be held by the same individual, such as when a recreational boat is towed in by the Coast Guard only to be given a ticket for improper safety equipment. Coast Guardsmen walk a fine line between cop and savior. One night at Group Moriches, I had to make a tough decision that really demonstrated this fine line Coast Guardsmen walk on a daily basis.

It was already very rough offshore when we got a call from a sailboat requesting to tie up at our dock for the night to get out of the weather.

"Coast Guard Group Moriches, this is the sailing vessel *Amy*. We are outside of Moriches Inlet and are taking a beating with this weather out here. We were wondering if we could come in and tie up at your station for the night. We don't have anywhere else to go and we're in pretty bad shape."

This is an unusual request, but I felt for them. I called the command duty officer and told him of the situation. He figured it would probably be okay for one night, and so we gave the boat permission to tie up at our dock.

"*Amy*, Coast Guard Group Moriches, roger that. You have permission to tie up here for the night. I need to get some information from you . . ."

The radioman ran through the standard questionnaire and got the personal information from the three people.

Since we had no real security back then, I realized these people would have free reign of the station while we slept. The only guy awake would be the radioman. I decided due diligence dictated that we run a criminal records check on them, as we do with many boardings.

"Hey, we better do an EPIC check on all of them just to make sure they're legit. I don't want some criminals running around the station at night while we're asleep."

"Roger that," said the radioman as he dialed up the El Paso Intelligence Center. About twenty minutes later the radioman came to the doorway between the radio room and the operations center with a telling grin on his face.

"Are you ready for this?" he asked. "Two of them came back clean. The operator of the sailboat is a convicted felon and a deserter from the U.S. Army."

"Holy shit. Are you kidding me?"

"Nope," he said, nervously half-laughing.

"Did you do the pre-boarding questionnaire?"

"Yep."

"Do they have any weapons on board?"

"They have one rifle and two handguns."

"Shit!"

The boat crew was down at the dock helping them tie up by this time. I had a big dilemma. Were these nice boaters who just requested assistance from their friendly neighborhood Coast Guard, or were they criminals who were going to conduct a mass murder on us while we slept? If it had just been me on my own, I would have had the luxury of giving them the benefit of the doubt, but I was responsible for the lives of all the guys on duty that night.

With a sense of excitement about the drama unfolding, smiling, I said to the radioman, "What are we gonna do?"

"I don't know," he said smiling back and shaking his head. He trusted that I would figure out what to do.

Something had to be done. I had followed protocol and I was already aware of the information. I couldn't undo that. This guy had to be arrested. After all, he's the one who asked to tie up to a Coast Guard station. I still felt bad about having to do it.

Conducting a federal arrest is an involved process, especially in the middle of the night. It is much easier to have the arrest made by local authorities, but for that there must be local charges.

"Get the boat crew up here as soon as they're done tying up his boat."

A short while later the boat crew came into the operations center fresh from the dock with ruddy faces and wearing orange float coats. They were wondering what was up.

"The operator of the sailboat is a convicted felon and deserter from the Army."

"What!?"

"I don't feel good about it, but the dumb-ass shouldn't have asked to tie up here. What was he thinking? Our hands are tied. Like it or not, we know about it now and we have to act on it. I don't want to have to do a federal arrest on this guy. We need to figure out a way for the locals to take him."

That's when one of the boarding officers spoke up, "It's against New York State law for a convicted felon to possess a firearm."

"That's it. Good call. I'll call Suffolk County and see what they say."

I called the Suffolk County Police Department who found it to be an unusual cross-jurisdictional situation. They were concerned with getting a warrant to search the boat and how we would tie the firearms to the felon. I reminded them of the Coast Guard's authority to conduct boardings, and we agreed to a plan.

While I mostly thought this was just an unfortunate situation that was going to end badly for the sailboat operator, the possibility that they could start shooting at us at any time lingered in the back of my mind.

The Suffolk County police officer arrived a while later making sure to keep his vehicle out of view of the sailboat. The policeman and I stood inside the door of the boathouse looking out down the pier. Since the Coast Guard's legal ability to search a vessel is broader than that of local police, I had my boarding team conduct a boarding of the sailboat.

"We're going to conduct a standard Coast Guard boarding of your boat. Would you folks mind stepping onto the dock while we do it?" They complied without complaint, happy to be safely moored and out of the heavy weather.

"Where are the weapons you reported?"

"Down below in the cabin."

"Ok, I'm going to remove them for officer safety, ok?"

"Sure, no problem."

With that, the boarding officer went below and emerged with the weapons in hand. He asked the sailboat operator, "Are these your weapons?"

"Yes, they are mine," he replied.

The boarding officer then signaled to the police officer and I as we looked on from inside the boathouse. The policeman then walked down the dock and placed the sailboat operator under arrest for being a convicted felon in possession of firearms in the State of New York.

Sometimes, when placed in a position of leadership tough decisions must be made. As bad as I felt having to do that, I would have felt much worse having to explain to the wives of the crew why I let a wanted, convicted felon with weapons shoot their husbands while they slept. Unfortunately, there was nothing but resentment for the Coast Guard left amongst that sailboat crew after our good-intentioned attempt at charity.

Fortunately, the rewards of running search and rescue cases far outweighed any negativity associated with law enforcement. Of all the cases I was involved in during my twenty-year career, one stands out as the ultimate example of what is possible when a team strives for excellence and pays attention to detail.

"Coast Guard, Coast Guard, come in Coast Guard."

"Vessel calling Coast Guard, this is Coast Guard Group Moriches, channel one-six, over."

"Coast Guard, this is the *Jenny L.* I just picked up a man in the water who's been out here for two days, and he says his captain is also out here too somewhere, over."

"*Jenny L,* Coast Guard Group Moriches, roger. What is your position, over?"

"My position is 41 degrees, 31.4 minutes north; 075 degrees, 47.2 minutes west. I'm headed for Moriches Inlet now with the man. You might want to call an ambulance. He's in pretty bad shape."

I had just relieved the watch less than an hour before. So much for my hopes of a nice, quiet Saturday morning. From my vantage point at the operations center chart table, I had overheard the conversation the radioman was having and plotted the position as I heard it. The position plotted right in the middle of the Hudson Canyon, which is where the continental shelf drops off between New York and New Jersey. I had heard that was a good fishing spot for those recreational fishermen adventurous enough to go that far out. There was only one problem: the Hudson Canyon was almost 80 miles away, and if the *Jenny L* was actually there, we would not be able to talk to her because the VHF radios we were using only had a range of about 25 miles. I knew immediately the position was no good.

"Confirm that position; it can't be right."

The radioman asked the *Jenny L* to confirm the position where they had picked up the man in the water. The *Jenny L* said he had just headed out of Moriches Inlet to go fishing and about twenty minutes later he found the man. He estimated he was about seven and a half miles south of the inlet when he came across the man trying to swim to shore. The timing made sense based on the speed of a recreational boat, but the position was still unreliable.

"DF that guy," I told the radioman. This was not something the radioman of the watch ordinarily did. After a moment's hesitation, he realized what I was telling him to do and remembered that the VHF radio had a direction finder installed. He called the *Jenny L* and asked for more information. As the *Jenny L* transmitted, he switched on the direction finder that indicated a bearing of southeast from our Coast Guard station, which was directly across the bay from Moriches Inlet.

I didn't trust the position information coming from the *Jenny L.*

"Get another DF on that guy."

The *Jenny L* was heading in at full speed, but this time the DF showed a bearing of southwest of our station that when paired with the last bearing, did not make sense especially if he was heading straight for the inlet. It was critical to have an accurate position where the survivor had been recovered if we were going to be able to locate the other person in time. I knew the position we had was inaccurate. LORAN-C electronic navigation sets had a "man overboard" button to mark a position should someone fall overboard. They also allowed boaters to program in the coordinates of their favorite fishing spots, such as the Hudson Canyon. The operator of the *Jenny L* had inadvertently hit the fishing waypoint button instead of the "man overboard" button when they picked up the man. I knew I had to debrief this survivor in person or our chances of finding his captain out there were slim to none.

"Boston Rescue, Air Station Brooklyn, this is Group Moriches on the SAR-Tel."

Our "bat-phone" was a red telephone hanging on the wall. It was an open phone line between all operation centers in the First Coast Guard District. Whenever we needed a helicopter we would simply pick up the SAR-Tel and request a launch. All operation centers in the district could hear the brief as they all had the same set-up as we did, which included an old school, wood and fabric PA speaker box hanging on the wall.

"Boston's on."

"Brooklyn's on."

"Boston, Brooklyn, Group Moriches, we need a launch. We've got a man in the water approximately seven and a half miles due south of Moriches Inlet. One survivor has been recovered, but he claims there is one more out there. I'll have exact coordinates and search area parameters once you get airborne."

I plotted the direction finder bearing from our station, which was conveniently printed on the chart. Then I took my dividers and measured off seven and a half nautical miles. I put one point of the dividers on the jetties on the chart and the other point where it landed on the radio bearing. This was our best guess position. I picked off the latitude and longitude just in time.

"Group Moriches, Coast Guard Rescue 6586, airborne en route, three P-O-B, request you take my radio guard."

The radioman relayed the position to the helicopter along with the search directions I had issued: a vector search with quarter-mile track spacing. This search requires the helicopter to fly over the last known position many times on different vectors, while keeping within a quarter mile of the center. It was a shot in the dark, but for an initial search, it was the best we could do.

The radioman had called for the ambulance that must have been in the area, because it was soon on our dock. I knew the paramedics would immediately take the survivor away once the *Jenny L* arrived, so I told the radioman I was heading down to the dock to meet the boat.

When I got down to the dock, I made sure the ambulance driver understood they could not take the survivor away until I had debriefed him. Debriefing survivors by the SAR controller was not something that was usually done, or required. I could tell the paramedics weren't used to being told what they could or couldn't do with a patient, but they did not argue the point. The *Jenny L* arrived shortly thereafter and the paramedics transferred the survivor to the gurney.

I had to confirm the position where the crewmember was picked up. The owner of the *Jenny L* said he was 7.6 miles south of the Moriches sea buoy. When I asked him about the differing radio bearings we had on him coming in, he admitted that would be accurate because he had over-steered the inlet on the way in. That confirmed it for me: our initial bearing southeast of the inlet was accurate and his estimate of 7.6 nautical miles from the sea buoy would be all I had to go on.

I introduced myself to the survivor. He said his name was Tommy Flanagan and that he was the mate on the commercial fishing vessel *Seaspray* out of Hampton Bays, New York.

"My captain is still out there clinging to a hatch cover."

"When was the last time you saw him?"

"I guess about three hours ago. I've been swimming for about three hours. But you've got to find him soon. He's not going to make it much longer."

I explained we were going to do our best to find his captain and asked him to tell me exactly what happened from the beginning. These are the events as they were relayed to me.

At 9:00 a.m. on Thursday, July 4, 1991, the wooden commercial fishing vessel *Seaspray* got underway from its homeport of Hampton Bays, New York, and headed out of Shinnecock Inlet on a routine fishing trip. At approximately 10:30 p.m. that evening, just a few miles offshore, the captain and his only crewman noticed a fire coming from behind the engines in a wall adjoining the fishing hold. The crewman thought of calling on the radio, but the fire was thought to be electrical in nature and the power was going on and off. Some wax boxes against the wall in the fish hold caught fire, and they fought the fire from the opposite side of the wall in the fish hold. Although the fire was believed to be out at times, it re-flashed. And after expending six of their portable fire extinguishers, the captain and his crewman decided the fire was out of control.

They headed back up to the bridge only to find it totally engulfed in flames. With flames shooting out of the pilothouse door, the captain singed his face during a noble attempt to reach the emergency beacon, which had unfortunately been mounted inside the pilothouse. The captain, his crewman, and their dog mustered on the stern of the boat. The men donned survival suits and attempted to inflate the life raft with the foot pump. But in the choppy seas and on a deck crowded with equipment, the life raft was punctured during inflation.

Two-thirds of the vessel was now engulfed in flames and they were forced to abandon ship onto three wooden hatch covers the captain had thrown overboard. In the choppy seas, the dog was unable to balance on the hatch cover for long and was lost. The vessel burned for approximately four hours and sank.

The two men clung to the hatch covers throughout the night hoping that someone would have seen the fire from shore and reported it to the Coast Guard. If the flames were seen from shore, perhaps they were mistaken for some Fourth of July festivities, because it was never reported to the Coast Guard.

On Friday, July 5, 1991, the men noticed two vessels nearby and decided that each would swim to one of the vessels. The crewman remembers getting to within a couple hundred yards of one of the boats and he could see the people on deck. But when he tried to blow the whistle attached to his survival suit, he was too winded to make a noise, and the boat passed right on by. The captain and his crewmember were now separated. The crewmember eventually fell asleep on his hatch cover. When he awoke about five hours later, by some miracle, he found his captain still clinging to a hatch cover only fifteen feet away from him.

The captain's condition had deteriorated and the crewman had to stay awake all night holding his captain on the hatch cover.

After a second night at sea clinging to wooden hatch covers, at approximately 6:00 a.m. on July 6, 1991, the captain told his crewman that waiting to be rescued was of no use. He convinced his crewmember to try and swim to shore and save himself. The crewman reluctantly left his captain and began swimming toward shore. Approximately three hours and twenty minutes later, at 9:20 a.m., the *Jenny L* recovered the crewman.

"We'll do our best to find the captain," I assured the crewman, and released him to the ambulance driver. I ran back up the stairs, two steps at a time, to the operations center.

I had dispatched our twenty-eight foot rescue boat, Coast Guard Station Shinnecock's forty-one foot rescue boat, an eighty-two foot Coast Guard patrol boat from Fire Island, a helicopter from Coast Guard Air Station Brooklyn, and a large helicopter from Coast Guard Air Station Cape Cod. Now all I had to do was figure out where to send them, and fast.

The helicopter, as standard procedure, dropped a datum marker buoy in the water prior to commencing the search. Between searches, helicopters typically return to the datum marker buoy and pass the current latitude and longitude of the drifting buoy. This allowed search and rescue controllers to calculate the current set and drift, or direction and velocity of the current and wind leeway. We didn't have time to wait for the present marker buoy to drift enough to make calculations and so I decided to go with the historical data in the log.

I had decided a couple of years before that the drift information should be recorded for future search planning. I pulled out the government-issue, green record book I had previously marked "DMB Log," and found a number of entries, made mostly by me. Apparently, my three other controller colleagues didn't find it necessary to follow the lead of the junior zealot who had created more paperwork for them. I determined the average direction and velocity to be 0.6 knots due west.

I measured 7.6 nautical miles with my dividers and put one point on the chart symbol for the Moriches sea buoy, and I marked the point on the initial radio bearing line already marked on the chart. This point was our revised "last known position."

The first helicopter had completed the first search with no sign of the captain and headed in for a crew change. The forty-one foot boat from Station Shinnecock reported on the way to the search area that it was passing through the floating burnt debris that was the *Seaspray*.

A second helicopter was on the way to the search area. Its estimated time of arrival was approximately twelve o'clock noon. I calculated that was 2.7 hours since the crewmember had been recovered, which meant, based on our historical drift information, he could have drifted another 1.6 nautical miles due west. I measured off the 1.6 nautical miles and plotted the point due west of the last known position. This was my theoretical best guess of where the captain would be when the second helicopter got on scene.

Amidst so much uncertainty, normally a very large box would be drawn to make sure all possibilities were covered. However, due to the fact that we knew the captain was alive six hours prior, and that he was reported to be on his last leg, a surgical strike was called for. If the search area was drawn too small, he might have drifted out of that area already, and if the search area was drawn too big, he might be dead by the time the helicopter found him. I only added the smallest margin of error, a minimal distance west of my calculated datum, when I determined the search area. At that point Captain Jerry's guardian angel took a hold of my pencil-holding hand as I drew the "commence search point," and then the first leg at the western edge of the creeping line search.

Ten minutes into the search, the helicopter had completed the first leg and had turned 180 degrees back onto the second leg. Fourteen minutes into the search, halfway down the second leg, the helicopter flew right over Captain Jerry at low altitude.

"Group Moriches, Coast Guard Rescue 6552, we have the survivor in sight and are deploying the rescue swimmer at this time, over."

During an interview following the rescue, Captain Jerry explained how he realized he had nothing left. It was impossible to hold on any longer to the rolling hatch cover. He had made his peace with God, and was about to let go, roll off, and drown when he heard that distinctive sound of the Coast Guard helicopter. He looked up and saw the orange helicopter fly right over him.

The radioman ran out to the chart table and we exchanged celebratory high-fives. I released all of the other boats and helicopters to return to base. The controllers at the Coast Guard Rescue Coordination Center in Boston were truly impressed, as was my wife. There was no one else to tell. There were no calls from William Shatner to film an episode of the TV show "Rescue 911," just a couple of very proud and satisfied guys.

I was at home during the following Monday morning brief, when the officers gathered around the chart table to hear from the off-going Sunday controller what had gone on over the weekend.

"The weekend was pretty quiet; on Saturday Kevin had a couple of people in the water, but they were both recovered. All else was quiet."

"Great. Have a good day," was the response from the commanding officer and his staff as they picked up their coffee cups and headed back to their desks.

Captain Jerry was not supposed to die that day. As for me, I was honored to be on duty that morning with Captain Jerry's guardian angel.

Things changed for me during my last year at Group Moriches. A master chief boatswain's mate who was skipper of one of our eighty-two-foot patrol boats was reassigned to our office and was awaiting retirement. He was one of those boatswain's mates who had been in command for fifteen of the past twenty years of his career. He had spent most, if not all of those years on Long Island, and as a result he was a legend. At least, that's how he tells it. He was popular; that was a fact.

His name was Ed. His appearance contributed to the reason we referred to him as Special Ed when he wasn't around. He was medium height with a potbelly and Coke bottle glasses. It was a perfect nickname. He really was special, in many ways, both good and bad.

"Are you fuckin' kidding me? You know what I'm gonna do with this? Watch very closely," I heard the master chief say, in his heavy New York accent, as he dropped the stack of papers into the lieutenant's trashcan. I had just walked into my lieutenant's office to witness this act of disrespect. The lieutenant sat there behind the desk with wide eyes and a big grin. He would have found this routine even more amusing if he were not the brunt of it. They hadn't taught him at the Academy how to handle this type of character, so he decided not to handle him at all.

"That's what I think of your fuckin' emails," Master Chief said, turning to me with a smirk. He wasn't loud, just matter of fact.

"Can you believe it?" he said quietly while leaning into me and looking over his Coke bottle glasses. "A lieutenant trying to give me fuckin' emails to go through?" He knew exactly how far he could go with his stand-up routine, to avoid crossing any lines that might cause the lieutenant to get upset. Just the same, he left the emails in the trash for the lieutenant to retrieve. Master Chief was only half kidding and the lieutenant got the message quickly. Not only was he not going to be working for anyone his last year in the Coast Guard; he couldn't survive without someone working for him.

It wasn't long before the lieutenant called me into his office and told me that I was no longer going to be an operations center watch-stander and that he needed me as a day worker. This meant there would only be three guys in the rotation standing watch. They were not happy and neither was I, especially when the lieutenant broke the news that I would be working for the master chief.

"Listen, I'm going to whip your ass into shape. Got it?"

This is how Master Chief greeted me when I walked into the office he had been given down the hall from the operations center. I was a thirty-year-old man, with ten years in the Coast Guard, and was on the list for promotion to chief petty officer.

"Listen, go find a desk and put it right over there," he said pointing to the opposite corner of the same small office.

"Go find a desk?"

"Yeah, go find a fuckin' desk, now, and don't come back until you find one. Understand? Go!"

I turned with my mouth open and walked out of his office and started down the stairs, not exactly knowing where I was going, in more ways than one.

I wandered about asking anyone if they knew where I could find a desk. An engineer showed me an old garage behind the boathouse that I had never noticed before. Buried deep inside this garage was an old metal desk with about an inch of dust on it. The engineer was nice enough to help me lug it into the building and up the flight of stairs. Somehow I was able to preserve the cleanliness of the dress uniform I was wearing during this evolution.

"Good," said Master Chief. "Now get a pen and paper and start taking some notes."

And that's how I became a secretary for a boatswain's mate.

It was truly amazing to me that a guy could have such a huge ego and no shame for the things he would do. Sitting in the chair with his feet on the desk doing nothing he would say, "Hey, do me a favor. Get Jerry Heany on the phone for me." It's funny how he had the habit of always saying, "Do me a favor." Of course, it's only a favor if the person doing it has the option of saying no. "Get someone on the phone for me" might not sound too ridiculous until you realize that Jerry Heany's phone number was written on a sticky note stuck to the phone on his desk. He actually expected me to get up, dial his phone, and after Jerry answered, hand him the phone.

He refused to use a computer.

"Do me a favor. Print up all my emails and read through them and pick out the ones you think are important and throw the rest in the shit-can."

The favors were not always Coast Guard related.

"Hey, do me a favor. Go down to the front and break up those pallets they're throwing away and pile the wood in the back of my truck. I need it for firewood."

He once hosted a diving safety seminar and had me bring all the bagels and doughnuts. Then he got concerned that we may not have enough.

"Hey, do me a favor. Cut all the bagels and doughnuts into four pieces."

When it came time for his retirement, he spent six months planning an extravaganza for 500 people. He had me stuff and address all the envelopes, which I did.

"Great, now do me a favor. Get some stamps and mail them. The lieutenant will pay you back."

Although I thought Master Chief was ridiculous, I never got mad or disgruntled. The truth is I enjoyed coming home and telling my wife about the ludicrous things he would make me do.

I knew Master Chief was looking for a job after he retired, so when I saw an advertisement in a magazine for a high profile marine operations job on Long Island, I had to let him know about it.

"Master Chief, check out this job opening I found," I said, handing him the opened magazine.

"Oh yeah," he said as his eyes got wide reading it. "This is good . . . Do me a favor. Draft me up a resume. I'll get you all the stuff . . ."

CHAPTER / 13

Chief Petty Officer "On Leadership"

"**N**ow Chief Gilheany, your presence is requested in Admin, Chief Gilheany."

I was in the operations center at Group Moriches when I heard that pipe come over the loudspeaker. Even at shore units the Coast Guard keeps the tradition of making announcements, or "pipes" as we called them. They are called pipes from the shipboard tradition of preceding each announcement with a two-note call to attention on the boatswain's pipe. It was mid-1993, and I was an E-6, or first class petty officer. I had advanced quickly through the ranks by scoring high on exams, getting good marks and receiving awards. I had taken the chief's test and was anxiously awaiting the results. I recognized the voice as that of the chief yeoman in administration. He would have been the first to receive the advancement list. This was either a terribly cruel hoax, or very exciting news.

Making chief in the Coast Guard is a big deal. Chiefs, senior chiefs and master chiefs are considered senior enlisted personnel. Parts of the uniform are slightly different than those of the junior enlisted. Chiefs also share some of the privileges of officers. When piped, their presence is always requested, not ordered. On board ships, chiefs are assigned to staterooms and no longer have to live in the thirty-man berthing area. While officers gather in the wardroom to eat, relax, and socialize, chiefs also have their own space known as the chief's mess where no one, including officers, is allowed to enter without permission.

"What did he just say?" I asked the radioman on watch, to make sure I had heard it correctly.

"He said Chief Gilheany!"

I hurried down the stairs to the chief yeoman who showed me the advancement list message that had just come in with my name above the cut. According to this message, I was to be promoted to chief petty officer on July 1. I was very excited and so was everyone else. My wife and I celebrated and dreamed about returning to New Orleans to take the chief quartermaster billet as the operations center supervisor at Group New Orleans.

Unfortunately, my excitement turned into heartbreak when we found out the next day that the Coast Guard Institute had made an error with the advancement list. Headquarters ordered the Commanding Officer of the Institute to personally call every person on the list that was affected by the error. We were told that all the calls would be made the next day, and if we didn't receive a call by the end of the workday, that we would not be affected. The entire next day I awaited the dreaded phone call. The workday ended without a call. My wife and I celebrated once again over the exciting news.

The following day, at approximately 11:00 a.m., I received a call from the Commanding Officer of the Institute telling me that I was not above the cut, but quite a few names below it. I felt justified in expressing my displeasure, especially since I should have received that call the day before. The Commanding Officer was surprisingly apologetic and honest. He explained that their intention was to call everyone the day before, but they mistakenly started with the West Coast instead of the East Coast, so that by the time they got around to calling the East Coast personnel, the workday had ended. I couldn't believe that they had botched it twice, or that they had admitted it. I received a formal letter of apology from Headquarters, as did all the others affected. Each month we watched to see how many guys would make it before the list ran out at the end of the year. Luckily, I made chief on November 1.

"Hey, you fucking boot! So you think you're gonna be a chief?"

The hazing started by the other chiefs even before my official date of rank. The Coast Guard and Navy had a great tradition of initiating their new chiefs. I was given a green, hardback, ruled record book from the government stock system. This was my "charge book," which I was directed to carry with me at all times and warned never to let it out of my sight. Sometimes a charge book would have a hole through it with a heavy chain attached. Thankfully, mine was given to me without a chain. I was told that I must ask each chief I encountered to sign my charge book. After giving me a bunch of shit they would write things such as, "This dirt bag E-7 had the nerve to tell me he was CHIEF Gilheany. I hope, your honor, you deal with this scum of the earth accordingly." The charges would be read during the mock trial at the initiation, at which time, I was told I would be fined heavily for each one.

I never felt the need to participate in hazing myself. Simple teasing was my method of choice for sizing up a guy, but I was honored to go through this age-old tradition. It was not only because I didn't want to miss out on any tradition or experience, but I also understand that it serves a purpose. Observing a man's reactions to such events gives a crude glimpse into his character. The ones who endure the crucible honorably are accepted as brothers. I also understand many will never get that.

The Coast Guard in the early 1990s was in the process of "revamping" chiefs' initiations. Hazing was in the national spotlight and apparently some had complained. Thank God for the renegades of the Long Island East End Chief Petty Officer's Association, led by Special Ed, who were not interested in reforming themselves to this new way of thinking.

The chiefs at Group Moriches told me I had to go find as many chiefs as I could, get them to sign my charge book and shine all of their shoes. I got my shoeshine kit and headed on the road to Governor's Island Coast Guard base in New York Harbor where I found many chiefs. Some got into it, giving me a ration of shit and writing outlandish lies in my charge book. Others just congratulated me, welcomed me to the chief's corps, and wrote congratulatory notes. Very few allowed me to shine their shoes, although I offered it to each one.

One old Filipino master chief on Governor's Island refused to sign my book. Instead he lectured me for half an hour on the indignities of what I was participating in. I never ran into another guy like that in the Coast Guard, before or since. He had given this a great deal of thought and sounded like a wise old man. Perhaps he had a different frame of reference based upon life experience. I respected his opinion.

The following day I was told to report to the chief boatswain's mate at Station Eaton's Neck. This chief was not a nice guy, I could tell. I put up with his shit as required. At lunch time he told me, "Go up to the third deck and tell those seamen chow is ready."

"Okay, Chief."

I walked up the flights of stairs to the top and opened the door. I expected to see a tired bunch of nineteen-year-olds lying around watching *The Price is Right*. Instead, I saw a conference table full of officers in full dress blue uniforms. At the head of the table was Captain Thad Allen, the Commander of Group Long Island Sound. I stopped dead in my tracks.

"Sorry, Captain," I said as I quickly backtracked a step, still holding onto the doorknob.

"Hold it. Come back here," the Captain ordered. "You all are dismissed," he said to the group staff sitting around the table. I stood aside as the ten or so officers filed past me down the stairs for lunch. When they were all out of the room, I walked slowly toward the Captain. He had spotted the green record book in my hand and knew exactly what it was for. I was a little worried that he might be opposed to the old chief's initiation process and put an end to it for me.

"Come on over here and sit down."

We had a long talk about how his father had been a chief and how important chiefs were to the Coast Guard and how I should be very proud. He signed a congratulatory note in my charge book and wished me well. In 2006, Admiral Thad Allen would become the 23rd Commandant of the Coast Guard.

I was told I must make an elaborate costume for the initiation. I decided to go in full and piss them all off. I became Super Chief. Royal blue thermal long johns, red knee socks to pull over my Chuck-Ts, red boxing shorts, royal blue sweatshirt and red plastic cape. Styrofoam muscles bulged under the sweatshirt, a felt Super Chief logo on my chest and an elaborate replica of a Coast Guard chief's anchor insignia on the back of the cape. Four other "E-7 dirt-bags" and I were ordered to stand out in front of the American Legion Hall on Montauk Highway in full costume for hours waving at cars before the initiation.

I can't reveal the top-secret proceedings, but at the end we got cleaned up, and our wives, who were patiently waiting in another

For our chief's initiation on Long Island we were required to wave at passing cars on Montauk Highway. I'm "Super Chief" in the middle.

Photo credit: Josh Lawrence/ The East Hampton Star; 1993.

room for the foolishness to end, pinned on our chief's anchors in a nice, civilized ceremony. All the chiefs who had given us shit the past couple of months congratulated us and welcomed us.

It was one important step closer to that patrol boat command. But for now, we were headed home.

I was given a few Chief billets to choose from, and by some miracle, one of them was Coast Guard Group New Orleans as the operations center supervisor.

Moving from Long Island back to New Orleans was an experience. It was January of 1994, and on the day the movers came, I had to chisel four-inch thick ice from the entire driveway. My wife and I drove down in one car. Somewhere between Birmingham, Alabama, and I-10 the scenery turned from gray to green.

One of the first places we hit when arriving in town was Bud's Broiler on City Park Avenue. We ate our No. 4 burgers with chili and cheese, and took in the familiar surroundings we hadn't seen in four and a half years; we knew we had made the right choice to come home. It was where we both belonged.

We were settling into our new apartment on Catina Street, when on Friday, January 29, 1994, three days before the day I was to report aboard Coast Guard Group New Orleans, I received a phone call from my new unit.

"Chief, I know you don't have to report in until Monday, but there's a big exercise going on tomorrow that's going to affect the rest of your tour here, so you might consider coming out and observing it."

I agreed, and the following morning I boarded the Coast Guard Cutter *Point Sal* in the Mississippi River. The *Point Sal* was going to kick off the New Orleans High Capacity Passenger Vessel Response Plan Exercise that had been in the planning stages for the previous six months or more.

Gambling had recently come to New Orleans. The state had issued a number of gaming licenses to casino boats, which planned to operate around Algiers Point, a treacherous bend in the river at New Orleans. There were four casino boats, and due to an exclusive deal with Harrah's to be the only shore-based casino, these boats had to get underway. Everyone in the maritime industry thought it was a bad idea and increased the risk of a maritime disaster. To prepare, the Coast Guard had led efforts to develop the High Capacity Passenger Vessel Response Plan. Now it was time to exercise the plan and see how all the agencies performed.

The *Point Sal* was drifting in a predetermined position just below the Crescent City Connection Bridge. At the top of the hour, the Commanding Officer told the seamen on the back deck to get ready and then picked up the radio microphone. "This is a drill, this is a drill, this is the motor vessel *Natchez*. We have been hit broadside and are going down fast. We are abandoning ship without delay. This is a drill."

Off the back deck, I saw two seamen chucking orange-painted pieces of 2x4 lumber, the size of bricks, into the water as fast as they could. There were as many orange bricks as the amount of passengers authorized to be on board the paddle wheeler cruise boat, *Natchez*.

I listened intently to the radio as the responders checked in to fulfill their respective roles. Soon rescue boats were zipping around the river picking up orange bricks. Coast Guard helicopters would hover over a batch so the boats would know where to go pick them up. The bricks floated down river at three miles per hour, the average speed of the river current. As a rescue operation, everything seemed to go well as long as the orange bricks were obvious to the rescue units.

I kept waiting for the search and rescue controllers, the guys I was getting ready to be in charge of, to take control of the situation, calculate drift, and assign search areas. They never did. Once all the obvious bricks were recovered, as far as I was concerned, the operation fell apart. It never transitioned from a rescue operation to a search operation. Everyone else involved thought the exercise was a great success. When all the bricks were counted, it was determined that only 20 percent of them were recovered. When that number was reported in the media, it gave justification for the casino boats to violate their state licenses and refuse to get underway, because it was too dangerous.

I was disappointed, and I anxiously anticipated checking in on Monday morning to find out what was going on at this place.

"Hi," he said, extending his hand. "I'm Chief Lovett, and I'm incompetent."

He was about forty years old, this chief I was relieving. He was slightly pudgy, with a round face, goofy glasses, and a mustache. He was sitting at one end of a tiny office shared with the chief radioman. He did not get up. He sat there facing me, leaning forward with locked elbows and hands resting on spread knees. He had a grin on his face and I could tell he was a strange character.

"You're incompetent?"

"Yep, that's what they tell me. I'm not even allowed in the operations center anymore."

He was way too forthcoming with this self-deprecating news for my taste.

He had gotten into some trouble making operational decisions and had been banned from fulfilling his primary role of supervising the four E-6 watch-standers in the operations center. He had no shame left. He would be retiring soon and was just doing time.

Usually, when reporting aboard a new unit, time is taken to learn the way things have been done. By his own admission, I had nothing to learn from this chief. By the end of day two, I had found him a new location to occupy until his retirement and respectfully removed him from my new desk. Our main interaction over the next six months was joining him and his side-kick for lunch at Taco Bell, where they would, every day without fail, ask for encheritos, which didn't exist, and then laugh hysterically in tandem as the same poor woman behind the counter tried desperately not to roll her eyes.

All four of the E-6 first class petty officers I was now supervising had been senior to me a few months earlier, since their E-6 date of rank had preceded mine. I knew they would see me as a junior peer who got lucky on the chief's test, and that they would test me. For that, I was more than ready.

When I asked why they had not taken charge during the exercise, I was told that search and rescue didn't apply here because of the river and marsh. This myth was widely embraced by all but one of them, as it made their lives much easier to go along with it. I discussed some of my concerns with the lieutenant and was surprised at the response.

"Chief, have you had TQM training?"

"No."

"That's unbelievable. I don't know what you all have been doing up there, but the Coast Guard's on TQM now and you need to get on board. Here, read this book."

She gave me a book on TQM and ordered me to read it. The Coast Guard was going through changes during the 1990s: embracing Total Quality Management (TQM) and a number of other shifts that I liked to refer to as the corporatization of the Coast Guard.

I waited as long as I could before I started making changes, but we were in the business of saving lives. In the operation center I explained to the controller on watch that we would be doing a certain procedure a little differently.

"Chief, with all due respect, you can't tell us what to do anymore. We're on TQM. We have a Natural Working Group."

Biting my tongue, I quickly straightened him out on his misunderstanding of the program. I decided to attend one of their Natural Working Group meetings. Their sole agenda item was to decide which flavor of soft drink they wanted in the vending machine.

It wasn't long before they found out just how big a hard-ass I was. I had been told that my guys always wandered in late to the monthly all-hands meetings, in the middle of the Captain's speech. They wanted to get their watch relief over with before the meeting so the off-going guy could take off as soon as it was over. I made myself clear for the next all-hands day.

"Hey, tomorrow is all-hands. So don't relieve the watch until after it's over. I want both of you to be at the all-hands and relieve the watch when all-hands is over, OK?" After some hemming and hawing and attempts to change my mind, Josh, a blonde-haired Kentucky country boy, agreed. But I knew he was not going to do as I said.

The next morning after the morning brief, I said to Josh and Ted, "OK, let's go to all-hands, you can relieve the watch after." I walked out and headed down to the auditorium. Twenty minutes passed before they showed up in the middle of the Captain's speech. When it was all over and everyone went back to work, I went into the operations center and asked Ted, "So what happened?" Ted was a boatswain's mate who looked like he spent all his free time in the gym. He also didn't want to be in this job and was the one who resented me the most.

"What do you mean?"

"You didn't come to all hands like I told you to."

"Oh well, we just decided to get it done real quick. Josh was up all night and wanted to get out of here and stuff."

"You remember I told you not to relieve the watch and to come to all-hands, right?"

"Yeah, but . . ."

With that I flopped the Page 7, a service record write-up I had prepared, onto the top of the console.

"Okay, well, here's a Page 7 I need you to sign."

Ted couldn't believe it. He picked it up at arm's length, making it clear he was not accepting it, and read where I said he disobeyed a direct order.

"What? Are you serious?"

"Yeah, that's what happened, right? This is the military, right? I give you orders and you obey them, or you don't, and I document it with a Page 7 entry in your service record, right?'

I was very matter of fact and unemotional. He didn't know what to think.

"Well, I'm not signing that."

"Okay, no problem."

With that I flopped another Page 7 on the console. I leaned in and lowered my voice; "This is the same entry with a line below it stating that you refused to sign it. It's still going in your service record, and the next time you disobey one of my orders I'm going to do a 4910 charge sheet on you and send you to Captain's Mast, understand?" Captain's Mast is an old sailor term for commanding officer's non-judicial punishment, which includes the authority to impose reduction in rank, restriction to base, and the garnishment of wages.

I paused for a second, but didn't wait for an answer, and walked out of the operations center. Word spread quickly. Mission accomplished.

I had to convince the officers that the operation center was not functioning as it should be. Oddly enough, the officers in the command had no problem with these guys.

One guy in particular, Harry Morrissey, or "Coast Guard Harry," as friends and neighbors knew him, was their favorite.

He was a personable and popular guy. He had filled the vacuum since the previous chief had been fired, perhaps before that. He was the default leader of the four, if there was one.

One day while Harry was on watch, I heard him working a search and rescue case. I went next door into the operations center and got briefed on the case. A crew boat had removed a suicidal man from an oil rig and was bringing him back to shore. Unfortunately, the crew boat guys left the suicidal man unattended and wrapped in a blanket on the back deck. After about forty minutes they noticed he was no longer on board. Harry sent a helicopter to do a vector search around the crew boat's reported position.

This was improper procedure. The crew boat had been running for forty minutes at twenty knots. The man could have jumped off anywhere along the fourteen miles the boat had travelled since he was last seen. When I found out, I called for another helicopter to search the boat's track line. They found the blanket on the boat's track line about fourteen miles behind where the helicopter was searching. Had we done the proper search, would we have found the man? Maybe, maybe not, but regardless we were required to do the proper search. I thought this example would convince the commanding officer (CO) my concerns were legitimate and that I needed to have free rein to take corrective action. When I got through explaining this act of negligence, the CO responded, "OK, Chief, but we don't want change just for the sake of change."

Change for the sake of change? I had my work cut out for me.

I eventually won Harry over when I showed him a Page 7 I had drafted detailing all the instances where he did not follow my, or the Coast Guard's, directives including the botched suicide search. I showed it to him as a warning. He had never been held accountable before, always able to schmooze his way through. He wasn't a bad guy, and we eventually came to a good working relationship.

The lieutenant had little experience in operations and was happy to let me handle the operational duties. I was happy running the Coast Guard operations off Louisiana and Mississippi. Besides the lieutenant, who was the operations officer, there were three lieutenant junior grades in our department. I worked closely with these two ladies and one man, who jokingly referred to themselves as the Black Officers Club (BOC), of which I was made an honorary member. Although senior to me, I trained them all and they gladly let me run the operation. But some things were beyond my control.

As far as I was concerned, the four guys standing watch in the operations center had the most important jobs in the unit. I had instituted a rigorous qualification process and wrote a policy manual that laid out the best practice for every possible scenario. I made sure my guys used that manual every time. I reviewed every case folder each morning and provided feedback on yellow sticky notes. However, not everyone shared my opinion on the importance of the watch. Some officers decided that it was not fair that one first class boatswain's mate, who worked in the aids to navigation division, did not have to stand duty. I was told that Petty Officer Lowman would be standing watch in my operations center, and to get him qualified. Needless to say, Petty Officer Lowman and his boss were very much opposed to this decision. As a result, it was very difficult to get Lowman qualified, although we eventually did. His performance on watch was marginal at best. When I confronted him on issues related to the watch, he acted like he didn't understand anything. I had no leverage over him since he didn't work for me. Both his attitude, and that of his boss, was, "See, I told you I shouldn't be on this watch." It was a bad situation, and I told my lieutenant that Lowman really should not be standing the watch. Unfortunately, we were all proven right during a regretful incident.

One evening around midnight, Petty Officer Lowman received a call. It was from the captain of a tugboat moored at a dock on the river above New Orleans. The captain told Lowman that his relief hadn't reported aboard yet. Lowman didn't understand why this captain was calling the Coast Guard to report such a thing. The captain explained that he had called the relief captain's house and his mother said she dropped him off at the dock around 11:30 p.m. Lowman was able to pry out of this captain that he suspected his relief captain may have fallen in the river while trying to board the boat. With that, Lowman called the Air Station and asked for a helicopter search. Lowman assigned the helicopter to conduct a vector search of the river next to the boat. This went on for a couple of hours, but the helicopter found nothing and was released.

I came to work around 7:00 a.m. as usual and went to the operations center to get a brief on the previous night's case. I couldn't believe what Lowman had done.

The Mississippi River flows three miles per hour, on average. It can flow up to six miles per hour in high river stages. The river stage is published by the Army Corps of Engineers daily. Years before, I had obtained a table from the Corps showing the surface river current at any particular river stage. On any given day, the watch-standers could determine the surface river velocity for search planning. This was explained in detail in our policy manual and an important part of our training program. Lowman just didn't do it.

I immediately looked at the river stage message and determined the surface current to be 4.2 miles per hour. Based on the number of hours since the man was last seen, he could have drifted 35.7 miles downriver. I called the Air Station and asked for another flight. This was unusual, but they trusted me with the new information. I calculated the exact spot the man would theoretically be in when the helicopter reached the river, and passed it to the helicopter as the commence search point.

Five minutes before the helicopter arrived on scene, we got a call from a boat in the river. "Coast Guard Group New Orleans, this is the *Allie Marie*. We've got a body out here." They passed on the position of the body and I plotted it on the chart. It was within a half-mile of the position that I had calculated.

The man was still clinging to his duffle bag, which seemed strange after all those hours. The body was recovered and positively identified as the missing captain. I decided, out of curiosity, to call the coroner and asked him the time of death. The coroner informed me that captain had only been dead for about an hour when he was found. He had been alive all night floating downriver while our helicopter was flying circles around the tugboat miles upriver from him. This time I wasn't happy about being right.

CHAPTER / 14

Bagpipes, Blessings, and Bereavement

It was great to be back in New Orleans. My wife and I had missed four Mardi Gras seasons while on Long Island. So we got back into the swing of going to our old spot on St. Charles Avenue at Seventh Street, down the block from my old mansion apartment.

"Oh, here they come, watch."

I got excited when the Pipes and Drums of New Orleans came by. It was a rare treat since they were the only bagpipe band in town. My Italian wife was less excited.

Growing up in an Irish family in Manhattan, the St. Patrick's Day Parade on Fifth Avenue was a big event for us. When I heard the pipes passing I always felt a mysterious sense of exhilaration. I think of it as a "gift," and I definitely had it. Some people, like my wife, are indifferent about the bagpipes. Others claim they hate the bagpipes, although I find that hard to believe. But those who have "the gift" are filled with emotion by the sound. They cry, scream, hoot, holler, and basically can't get enough. Maybe it's in the blood. I remember asking my mother once, after a pipe band passed, if she thought I could learn how to play the bagpipes. "Oh, no. That takes years to master. You would've had to start taking lessons years ago," she explained. I was ten years old at the time, and I believed her. I didn't realize then that it was her way of saying we couldn't afford such things.

"Hey, I know that guy."

I recognized the drum major as Dave Johnson, a civilian employee of the Coast Guard's Marine Safety Office. I had worked with him on a number of tactical plans.

The next time I was with Dave, I mentioned that I loved the bagpipes and that I had always wanted to learn how to play. "Well, you're in luck," Dave told me. "The Pipe Major (lead piper) is Steve Young. He's a chief radioman at the radio station."

I realized that things were starting to line up. My sister, knowing my childhood fantasy, had bought me a practice chanter, a long, narrow, wooden kazoo-sounding instrument, as a gift during a recent visit to the Celtic Nations Festival in City Park.

I contacted Steve and started taking lessons. After six months I had learned the first five tunes on the practice chanter. Steve told me it was time to buy some pipes. Once I had my pipes they dressed me up and put me out on the street in parades. My drones, the tall pipes that sound the background tone, were plugged off to conserve my air supply.

Word spread fast that there was an Irish Catholic guy learning to play the pipes and the Ancient Order of Hibernians found me after a parade and pressed me into service as their piper. They even purchased a saffron colored kilt for me to wear to ensure I would not be mistaken for a Scottish bagpiper. I barely knew how to play then, and I wasn't much better when, as a favor to a family friend, I was on stage for *Brigadoon* at the Thibodaux Community Theater a mere eighteen months after taking my first lesson. It's a good thing the folks in Thibodaux didn't know what bagpipes were supposed to sound like. They were just happy to have a live piper.

Bagpiping soon became a major part of my life. In addition to the Ancient Order of Hibernians, I became the piper for many Irish organizations in New Orleans, such as the Irish Cultural Society, the New Orleans Rose, the Downtown Irish Club, and the Ulster Project. I gave lessons to thirty students, five of whom became pipers, including the sole piper for the New Orleans Police Department and the sole piper for the New Orleans Fire Department. I also played at many weddings and funerals, and sometimes played in the French Quarter as a street musician just for the fun of it. I was a member of the Pipes and Drums of New Orleans, played in many Mardi Gras parades and, eventually, formed my own band called The New Orleans Irish Pipe Band in support of all the Irish organizations of New Orleans.

It is truly a thrill to march down the street and pass through a crowd blessed with "the gift." They couldn't cheer louder if the Rolling Stones walked by. It is a powerful instrument.

Word spread in the Coast Guard as well, and people started to ask if I would play for Coast Guard ceremonies. Early in my career, I had seen a Coast Guard piper named Mike Mone, wearing a Coast Guard bagpiper uniform he had made, in a Coast Guard publication. I dreamed about how cool it would be to be a Coast Guard piper someday, and how cool it would be if the Coast Guard had its own pipe band. Inspired by Mike Mone's uniform alterations, I decided to go for it and wore the kilt with the Coast Guard uniform while piping at Coast Guard functions. I received some strange looks from other enlisted personnel, but no officer who could have stopped me ever said anything other than, "You sound and look great. Thank you."

Being a Chief may have had something to do with the fact that I was never challenged. Although I was a junior Chief, I still took the service wide exam for promotion as soon as I became eligible. After all, you never know.

"Good morning, Senior Chief," Vic said, as I walked into our office one spring morning in 1997.

Victor Tran was one of the best guys I ever worked with and was my assistant during my years as the operations center supervisor. He was a second class storekeeper, born in South Vietnam during the war. His family escaped during the fall of Saigon on a fleet of shrimp boats while being shelled as they left the harbor. Rescued at sea, they lived for a while in a refugee camp in Guam. Eventually another family sponsored his family and they settled in New Orleans along with many other Vietnamese families. It was truly a blessing to have Vic working with me during those years. He was a kindred spirit and an even bigger hard-ass than me.

"Senior Chief? What are you talking about?" I said.

I truly had no idea.

"The list is out. You made the cut."

"Are you shitting me?! Let me see that . . . Holy shit!"

I couldn't believe I was making senior chief (E-8) on July 1. I only had the minimum time in grade as a chief to sit for the exam. I hadn't studied at all for the exam, because I figured I was way too junior to be competitive. I found out I had the second highest score on the senior chief quartermaster exam. It must have been all of that studying I had done over the previous fourteen years. This was very exciting news, especially since I had also passed the officer in charge review board and was now certified for Coast Guard command afloat. My dream of commanding a patrol boat was getting closer. But first I had to learn an important lesson.

For years I had been running the operations of Coast Guard Group New Orleans, even though my actual billet was just to supervise the four to five controllers who stood watch in the operations center. The operations officer was glad to allow me to write all operation orders, run all tactical planning conferences, and conduct briefings. I took my responsibility perhaps too seriously as a senior enlisted to mentor junior officers. I would get frustrated when junior officers failed to progress despite my best efforts. My frustration with some Coast Guard people, and with my mother and sister who had moved to New Orleans and were not happy, was taking its silent toll.

"Sweety!" I called to my wife, having decided it was time to go.

She didn't say one thing as she ran to my bedside. She could hear it in my voice.

"Let's go to the emergency room."

My wife, surprisingly good in emergencies, sprang into action like a well-drilled Coast Guardsman and didn't ask any questions until we were well underway.

Earlier that afternoon we had been eating brunch with my in-laws at the Beau Rivage Casino in Biloxi. I hated all casinos, and I hated the fact that my mother-in-law was a gambling addict. As I ate, I felt a pain in the left side of my chest. I tried to breathe deeply and relax so it would go away. It didn't. I realized my heart was racing. Maybe it's nothing, I thought. Then the pain started shooting through my chest and into my left arm, a symptom I only associated with a heart attack. I prayed and said nothing.

After the hour and a half drive home I got in bed and tried to relax. The scariest part was thinking I could control it with my mind, and then realizing the fact of my own powerlessness. Indeed, the more I thought of it, the worse it got. My heart was racing—pounding. Inside the emergency room, they gave me an EKG and did some blood work. The doctor asked how many hours a week I worked. I had never given that any thought before and did the calculations in my head.

"Sixty hours," I said. It wasn't until I said it that I realized it was a lot.

"There's nothing wrong with your heart, no signs of heart attack. You are suffering from stress."

The doctor gave me a thirty-day subscription for beta blockers, and told me to go see someone about managing my stress.

The beta blockers were a miracle cure. My heart went back to beating normally almost immediately. As the doctor ordered, I decided to go see the Coast Guard wellness people, whom I usually avoided. They gave me a workbook called a "Stress Map." I answered all the questions, and in studying the results I learned a very valuable lesson. I was stressed out due to how I dealt with my mother, sister, in-laws and some junior officers.

The lesson was that it was not their fault; it was mine. I was trying to control everything and was stressed out when I couldn't. I was a control freak.

I took the lesson to heart. I needed to let go of what I could not control. I had to accept that I could not "fix" everyone who I decided needed fixing. Many years prior, my mother had embroidered and framed the Serenity Prayer, which hung on a wall in our house. I always heard the prayer was associated with Alcoholics Anonymous, but as I read it again I realized it really should be "the control freak's prayer."

This was a significant event in my life. As of this writing, I have not had another incident since I learned to accept the things I cannot change. It's a good thing, too, because things got even more stressful for a while.

"Hey Chief, did you hear Harry slipped in the head and cracked his skull?"

"Really? Is he hurt bad?"

"There was blood to clean up."

When I spoke to "Coast Guard Harry" he said it was due to a leaky sink that was supposed to be fixed by the guys in public works. I called down to the public works guys and explained the situation, but they assured me the sink was recently fixed. I had them come check it out anyway. There was no leak to be found. A couple of days later the mystery was solved. We heard that Harry had fallen in the street while walking with his wife and she rushed him to the hospital. A CT scan revealed that Harry, a thirty-seven-year-old father of three, had a golf ball-sized malignant brain tumor.

A few days later I was there when Harry was wheeled into the operating room. The surgeon decided it was best not to try and extract the entire tumor, but to kill the rest of the cancer with radiation. I visited Harry regularly during this ordeal. He kept his spirits up throughout, but it was a bad prognosis. As his situation deteriorated, the decision was made to medically retire Harry so that his family would get full benefits upon his death.

I was in charge of Harry's retirement ceremony and worked closely with our commanding officer, who took a personal interest in the matter. By this time I had been playing the pipes for a couple of years, and Harry, being of Irish descent, asked that I play at his retirement ceremony. Although I had played the pipes for official Coast Guard events before, this was special. I decided Coast Guard pipers should have official permission for wearing a kilt and this seemed like a perfect opportunity to request it. On September 8, 1997, I wrote to Coast Guard Headquarters requesting permission to wear a Coast Guard bagpiper uniform for Harry's retirement ceremony. Although my request was endorsed by my commanding officer and the Eighth Coast Guard District office, Headquarters responded that while my request was honorable and one of a humanitarian nature, it did not constitute a legitimate exception within the limits of the uniform regulations. The letter went on to offer a glimmer of hope, however, by suggesting that a viable exception to the uniform regulations could be made if I requested to be designated an Official Coast Guard Bagpiper. On September 24, 1997, I wrote to Headquarters requesting to be designated an Official Coast Guard Bagpiper. Harry's retirement ceremony was two days later. I once again wore the kilt without permission or opposition, and I never did receive a response to that request to be designated an Official Coast Guard Bagpiper.

On the day of Harry's ceremony, we gathered in the auditorium space. Harry was confined to a wheelchair and could barely communicate or move. Harry had been a quartermaster. When he needed to use the bathroom before the ceremony, I quickly realized that it was up to me and another old quartermaster to assist him to the bathroom and from the wheelchair to the toilet. I remember each of us standing on either side of Harry in the stall making small talk while we waited for him to finish. I could never have anticipated this turn of events when I first met Harry a few years before. A couple of weeks later, Coast Guard Harry was dead.

This was a sad and stressful time for all of us, but it helped put things into perspective. Little did I know that in this time of sadness, my greatest blessing lay just around the corner.

In January of 1998, I was sitting with the Officer in Charge of Coast Guard Station New Orleans in his office adjacent to the New Canal Lighthouse on the south shore of Lake Pontchartrain. His phone rang and he answered it. It was the seaman on watch.

"OK, he's here with me, put it through. It's for you," the Officer in Charge said, looking surprised and reaching the receiver across his desk toward me. I immediately got nervous. Who even knew where I was?

"Hello?"

"Sweetie?"

My stomach sank. My wife never called me and would have had to track me down to find me. I could tell she was crying.

"What's wrong?"

"I'm pregnant," she said trying to hold back the tears.

At first, I was relieved that the house hadn't burned down. Then it sunk in. We had been trying to have a baby for seven years. We were at the point where we were considering going to what I referred to as "the baby store." Stefanie had gotten pregnant only once during that period, which ended in a miscarriage at eleven weeks.

We were very excited about this pregnancy, but my self-defense mechanisms were strong. I tried not to let myself really believe it was going to happen. The pain of the previous miscarriage was still with us. We vowed not to tell people.

As the weeks passed without incident it got more real. My wife told me she had an appointment with the doctor who was going to try and listen for a heartbeat.

I have only one regret in my life: I didn't even consider going with her. I had this foolish, self-imposed loyalty to the Coast Guard, where I thought they couldn't afford to be without me for a day. The old saying, "your wife didn't come in your sea bag," was still part of my mentality. Perhaps I was afraid. In any case, I didn't go and really didn't think I would miss anything. As soon as Stefanie told me she heard the heartbeat, I realized what a fool I had been.

That was the day the ghost of Harry Chapin started haunting me. When I was a kid, growing up without my father around, the song "Cat's in the Cradle" was popular. It was about a Dad who never made time for his son and ended up a lonely old man. As a young boy, the song made me sad but not because I related to the son wanting his Dad. I don't know why, but I felt sorry for the Dad for having squandered his great privilege of fatherhood. I felt like that Dad on that day, long before our baby was ever born. I vowed never to be like him again.

Emma, the greatest blessing of our lives, came to join our family on October 20, 1998. Because she was so perfect, we decided to quit while we were ahead. So, in addition to being Daddy, I also happily played the role of the pesky sibling she never had.

We learned a saying in boot camp: "Not in my Coast Guard." Most people probably blew that off as just a saying. Not me. "My Coast Guard" was this idea I had in my head of how I thought the organization should be. Unfortunately, sometimes people get in the way of ideals—some people slipped through the cracks.

"Hey, did you hear Chief Austin is going to be the new chief radioman?" said one of the radiomen. "He's buddies with the new CO we're getting. I hear they play golf together at the Navy base."

I didn't know either of them and didn't really care too much about it. On the day when Chief Austin reported in, he continually walked past me; making it obvious he was deliberately avoiding acknowledging my presence. I didn't know what his problem was until one of the radiomen told me that Austin thought he was going to be the top dog, until he found out I was making senior chief at the same time he was reporting in. I had never run into such a strange and petty character before. Give me a good ole' swaggering boatswain's mate any day! For the previous three years I had shared an office with the chief radioman. This new creepy chief, upon reporting aboard, moved his desk from our office to the back of the radio room. I don't think we said two words the entire year. His final act of resentment, though, would be talked about for years after.

In January of 1998, I finished my ten years of night school and received a Bachelor of Science in biology from the University of the State of New York. A few months later, I found out that I had been selected for promotion to chief warrant officer. I had a big decision to make. I had to decide whether I wanted to remain in the operational Coast Guard and continue to pursue my dream of command of a patrol boat. While I had all the qualifications, the odds weren't good. There was only one patrol boat billeted for a chief warrant officer in the entire Coast Guard. My other choice, typically offered to warrant officers with less than sixteen years in the Coast Guard, was to switch to the marine safety side of the Coast Guard and become a marine inspector.

I was commissioned as a chief warrant officer on July 1, 1998.

As early as 1838, the U.S. adopted laws to protect passengers from the dangers of vessels propelled by steam. After a series of disastrous events involving steamboats, such as boiler explosions and fires, more laws were passed in 1871. The agency then was known as the Steamboat Inspection Service. In 1932, the Steamboat Inspection Service merged with the Bureau of Marine Inspection and Navigation. During World War II, a presidential executive order temporarily transferred the Bureau of Marine Inspection and Navigation to the control of the Coast Guard. On July 16, 1946, this transfer was made permanent.[38]

The marine safety side of the Coast Guard is a regulatory agency for the commercial maritime industry. Coast Guard marine inspectors inspect all aspects of commercial ships for regulatory compliance. While operational folks usually mocked the marine safety side of the Coast Guard, it was understood that it could lead to lucrative employment after retirement. I thought about it long and hard. I decided to become a marine inspector, abandoning my dream of command. I realized that perseverance toward a goal is good, but knowing when to change course is just as critical. We were given orders to Coast Guard Marine Safety Office New Orleans. We bought our first house and prepared for our new life with Emma.

The creepy chief radioman that wanted to be king was even more disgruntled at my good fortune. He couldn't wait for me to leave and for the new commanding officer to arrive. The junior officers who I worked with were terrified that I was leaving. I had been running all the operations and they were going to be left in the lurch. My relief, a chief quartermaster from Mobile, Alabama, was old school and had no intention of doing the "officer's work" I had done. When asked by our junior officers if he would report in early so I could train him, he refused. Our junior officers tried to go over his head by requesting the Mobile

command release him early, but they refused. The junior officers were desperate, and without telling me, they asked my new
Marine Safety Office command to send me back to train the new
chief after I had reported in. They agreed. I was aggravated, but I
understood they were desperate.

We had our change of command and the new commanding
officer took over. I was promoted to chief warrant officer on July
1, 1998. I reported to the Marine Safety Office, and they sent me
right back to the Group to train the new chief. It was awkward to
say the least. I returned to my office and started going over stuff
with the new chief quartermaster.

At one point I walked into the operations center. The creepy
chief radioman walked by me, looked surprised, and kept going into the radio room. He came back out almost immediately,
passed through the operations center and kept going.

"Hey, sir, I just want to let you know . . ." it was one of the
radiomen. They liked me and hated their creepy chief.

"What's up?"

"Chief just came in here and asked me, 'What's fucking
Gilheany doing here?' "

"He said that?"

I found it hard to believe that this guy was so resentful of
me for no reason. Never mind the fact that he would refer to an
officer that way.

Back in my office a few minutes later, Rakisha, the panicking
junior officer who had desperately orchestrated my return, came
into our office with her arms folded and on the verge of tears.

"I'm sorry, Kev. The Captain just called me into his office and
asked me what you were doing here."

Apparently, that's where Creepy Chief was heading when he
ran past me in the operations center a few minutes before.

"I told him I worked it out for you to come back and train your relief, but he said to tell you that you are no longer welcome here and to escort you off the base."

I stood there with my mouth open. She was serious. After four years, two promotions, and a commendation medal, I was being escorted off the property in front of all my guys. I picked up my stuff and walked out. Rakisha escorted me to my car apologizing the whole way.

While disgusted, I was relieved to get out of there and move on.

CHAPTER / 15

9/11 – Operation Noble Eagle

"**G**ilheany, get in here!"

It was my boss, a usually quiet lieutenant commander who had been in the marine inspection business for a long time. I jumped up from the big wooden table in the front of our office space and walked over to his door. We were operating out of a small rental office in a business park in suburban New Orleans next to the river.

"Yes, sir?"

"What is this?" he said, showing me the CG835 ticket that I had written on a barge the previous day. I explained why I wrote it hoping my explanation would satisfy an inclination on his part that I had botched my first solo barge inspection.

I had been at the unit for six months and had been breaking in as a tank barge inspector. The bosses had decided to let me do my first solo barge inspection the day before. I gathered up my catalog case of the Code of Federal Regulations (CFRs) and headed up the river road a mile or so to a tank barge company along the bank of the Mississippi. I had been there a time or two beforehand while breaking in. The industry representative for the barge company had been dealing with new Coast Guard inspectors for years. He knew the regulations better than most inspectors. I looked at the warning sign on the barge and immediately noticed it did not say "Dangerous Cargo." I told the company man that I thought it should say dangerous cargo, and that I would look it up to make sure. I always carried that big black case of CFRs. Before the electronic age, marine inspectors were referred to as "bag carriers."

The company man assured me his sign was fine and that we should move on. I told him I would gladly look it up. After a few minutes of back and forth, he asked me to just write it up so we could move on. That's where I screwed up. I wrote the CG835 ticket for the company to get a new sign with "Dangerous Cargo" on it, without looking it up.

My boss was not impressed with this explanation.

"It's not supposed to say 'Dangerous Cargo.' Look it up."

I scrambled through the CFRs only to find that there are two kinds of signs depending on the type of cargo. The only difference is, one sign also says dangerous cargo and the other does not. Otherwise, the entire wording on the signs is the same. I felt horrible. Not just because I screwed up, but also because I had caused the company to spend money unnecessarily.

"Yeah, I screwed up. Sorry about that," I told the boss. "I should have looked it up. But the good news is the new sign still has all the wording required by the regulations."

"Wrong answer. Go back there, tell him you screwed up, and tell him to put the correct sign back on the barge."

I paused for a second or two in shock and said, "Yes, sir."

I got back in the government vehicle and drove back to the tank barge company rehearsing what I was going to say. I met with the company man and apologized profusely. It was bad enough I made him buy a new sign, but now I was going to make him buy another sign that matched the one I made him remove. Luckily he was used to new Coast Guard inspectors.

"Don't worry about it. I knew you were wrong. I've got the old sign right over there."

I remembered what my first chief taught us on the *Bear*, to always look things up for ourselves. That would be more important than ever in this job. I resolved to never make that mistake again and always looked up regulations no matter how sure I was. As a result, I became an expert and a very good inspector. So much so, that after retirement I was able to turn that expertise into a successful consulting business, and that same tank barge company became a good client.

I went on to become qualified to inspect the hull and machinery of all kinds of vessels, including the few steamships left in existence. I enjoyed the job even though it required dirty, hot, dangerous work. Day in and day out, we put on coveralls and crawled through nasty voids, double-bottoms, and cargo tanks. Sometimes it reached 130 degrees inside the tanks. Once a vessel passed inspection, we issued a Certificate of Inspection and it was legal to operate. That was the bad part. But the good far outweighed the bad. The New Orleans office was responsible for inspecting all U.S. flag vessels in the Caribbean, as well as Central and South America. I traveled to places as far away as Peru, Brazil, Trinidad, and Venezuela. Life was good.

Then the whole world changed in a single morning.

The phone rang as we were finishing our coffee and deciding who was going to do which jobs that day. I answered the phone. It was Lieutenant Commander White from the downtown office.

"Turn on the TV. A plane hit the World Trade Center!"

I turned on the TV and saw the North Tower of the World Trade Center in New York billowing smoke. We thought it must have been an accident with a small commuter plane. A few minutes later, we saw a second plane fly into the South Tower and we knew we were under attack. It was hard to believe it was really happening, but then both of the buildings collapsed. I remembered my wife and I had been on the roof of one of those towers with my father just a few years earlier. I was glued to the TV for the rest of the morning thinking about the horror of it all and what it would mean for the future.

"Alright, turn off the TV. Regular workday."

It was our supervisor. He was torn between succumbing to the world-changing events happening before our eyes, and the need to wrangle a bunch of warrant officers back into the standard Coast Guard routine. As if some senior person was going to come in and catch us watching TV during the workday. He didn't get it. I thought he was ridiculous. My world had changed in an instant, and his had not. It's funny how people react to events. Maybe it was because it was all happening five miles south of where I was born and raised.

I called my childhood friend back in Manhattan to see if everyone was okay.

"Andre, this is Kevin Gilheany. How's it going up there? I just wanted to check in and make sure everyone is okay."

"Yeah, well, I wish I could tell you that, but Mike Armstrong was in the Trade Center. He worked for Cantor Fitzgerald."

Cantor Fitzgerald's offices were in the north tower above the point of impact.

"No shit?"

"Yeah, it's fucked up."

Mike Armstrong went to grammar school with us at St. Ignatius Loyola at 84th and Park. He was a year behind us, and his brother was a year ahead of us. His father was the super-intendent of a building at 85th and Fifth. The Armstrong family lived there in the super's apartment, which was typically in the basement. The Armstrongs were one of many Irish families in Yorkville whose lives centered around St. Ignatius. Mike was the kind of kid, maybe the only kid, who didn't get picked on. Everyone liked him. He was always smiling; you couldn't get his goat if you tried. As if it weren't tragic enough, I found out that Mike Armstrong had recently gotten engaged to be married.

Andre lived in a high-rise building in lower Manhattan by the East River.

"I was sitting at my kitchen table eating a piece of toast and I looked downtown and saw the building on fire. I kept eating my toast trying to figure out what happened. I kept seeing stuff fall from the buildings and finally realized the stuff falling was people. I turned on the TV and saw what was happening. Then I ran downtown to get my son out of school because I didn't know what was going to happen next."

I went to see my department head.

"Commander, I want to volunteer for whatever the Coast Guard is going to do in response to this attack. I'm ready to go anywhere and do anything."

A few days later I got my wish. There was concern that a ship entering the U.S. could have people or devices on it that could do harm to major U.S. cities. Large Coast Guard cutters were reassigned to patrol the approaches to major ports around the U.S. One 270-foot cutter was assigned to the LOOP (Louisiana Offshore Oil Port), which is an offshore port for offloading su-pertankers into a pipeline. The LOOP is located approximately twenty miles off the Louisiana coast. The cutter was assigned to protect the LOOP and send boarding parties to board ships entering the Mississippi River bound for New Orleans and Baton Rouge. Large Coast Guard cutters usually conducted drug, fisheries, or migrant patrols. Boarding large commercial ships was not part of their routine. The cutter's boarding teams were going to be augmented with Coast Guard marine inspectors who had experience with large commercial ships. I was the third Marine Safety Boarding Team Leader to be deployed in the months after 9/11. There was a young, unqualified, lieutenant junior grade (O-2) assigned to me for this mission. After a briefing, we took the government vehicle and drove from New Orleans to Venice, Louisiana, at the mouth of the Mississippi River. The direction we received regarding this mission was less specific than I would have preferred. The operation was called Noble Eagle. During the mission briefing, much to the annoyance of my superiors, I asked many questions regarding the intent of the operation and what procedures ought to be employed during the boarding. The mission was new to everyone, and many of the answers were vague. Although these exact words were probably not used, the impression I got from my superiors was, "handle it." I was okay with that. Coast Guardsmen are often called upon to handle unusual situations with minimal guidance. I understood the intent of the mission. We needed to make sure nothing and no one harmful would be getting into the U.S.

During our drive down to Venice, I told the young officer assigned to me what we were going to do during the boarding, such as search for dangerous substances and devices, verify all on board had been cleared through intelligence, and search for any evidence that might indicate an association to terrorist organizations. Unfortunately, the young officer had different ideas. He decided to lecture me on the billions of peaceful Muslims in the world. Furthermore, he thought we were going out there to do a standard Coast Guard foreign vessel boarding and check the steering, etc. I was unsuccessful in convincing him. We agreed to disagree, and I was glad, for the sake of the country, that I was in the lead and not him.

When we arrived in Venice at the heliport usually used for transporting workers to oil platforms offshore, we waited a short while until our orange Coast Guard helicopter landed. It was the smaller of the two types of Coast Guard helicopters at the time, and state of the art compared to the museum piece I had flown in years before. We landed on the flight deck of the Coast Guard Cutter *Thetis*, which was patrolling out by the LOOP. The *Thetis* was the same class as the *Bear*, and I looked forward to reminiscing as I walked around the ship.

Almost everything about the ship was the same as the *Bear*, but it was a different experience being on board as an officer. I was assigned to an officer's stateroom and ate my meals in the wardroom with the rest of the officers. Wardroom protocol is traditional and rigid. All seats at the table are assigned according to rank, with the Captain at the head of the table. The most junior officers, warrant officers, sat at the far end of the table. Seamen, known as wardroom mess cooks, waited on us. The Captain was served first; we were served last. I was happy to have experienced this part of shipboard life for the first time. When I was promoted to chief warrant officer three years prior, I had to attend a mandatory school at the Coast Guard Academy. It was jokingly referred to as "knife and fork school" because they teach all forms of table manners and etiquette. Truth be told, that was the only part of the school I found useful. Despite this training, however, I did commit a faux pas in the wardroom. One night when the Captain was relaxing after the meal, he made some comment, which I responded to. All of a sudden it got very quiet and they all looked at me. Apparently, I wasn't supposed to speak unless called upon. Unregretful, I repeated that faux pas many times during my two weeks on board.

Ships arriving at the Southwest Pass of the Mississippi River were evaluated and prioritized. There were too many ships to board every one. Soon it was time for our first boarding. We had been told to try not to impede commerce and to let the ships proceed at a slow bell while boarding. The seas were about four to six feet as the boarding team mustered on the stern of the cutter near the small boat. I was the senior boarding team member and I briefed the boarding team on what we were going to do. We climbed into the small, orange, rigid hull inflatable boat. Despite the sea state, the boatswain's mate coxswain of the small boat pushed the throttles forward as far as they could go. It is said that boatswain's mates know only two speeds, full speed, or full stop. Off we went bouncing from swell to swell, squatting down to minimize our center of gravity and clinging tightly to the handgrips on the top of the orange pontoons. Salt spray covered us. We approached the ship, and I did not like what I saw.

There are two types of ladders to board ships. One is an accommodation ladder, which is an aluminum staircase, the top of which is fixed to the main deck. Underway, the bottom of the ladder is hoisted up to the main deck and secured. When it is needed, the bottom of the staircase is lowered to the water's edge. This allows boarders to walk up the suspended staircase along the side of the ship. The other type of ladder is called a Jacob's ladder. It is a rope ladder with orange plastic rungs tied into it. The Jacob's ladder is simply dropped down the side of the ship for boarders to climb. The ship had dropped the Jacob's ladder for us, but in the worst possible place. The ship was empty and riding high out of the water. The Jacob's ladder was lowered far back aft where the hull curves in toward the propeller. The bottom ten rungs or more were not even lying against the side of the ship. The ladder was dangling and swinging freely in the air. To make matters worse, we could see the top of the propeller turning about thirty feet aft of the dangling ladder as the ship moved forward slowly toward the sea buoy. If any of us fell off the ladder our life preserver would keep us afloat long enough for us to be chopped up by the turning propeller. I regretted not having gone to the bridge of the cutter and asserting myself so that this situation could have been avoided. The coxswain timed his approach to match the speed of the ship and positioned us close to the ladder. Timing was critical. Our boat was rising and falling four to six feet in the seas, but the ladder was not. I remembered that my buddy who had been out a few weeks before had warned me of this. He had timed his attempt incorrectly and grabbed the second to last rung by mistake. The bottom half of his body was dangling. When the next swell came, he was up to his chest in the water with all that equipment on. Luckily he was built like a fireplug, and as a former diver he was able to climb the bottom of the dangling rope ladder with just his arms.

I could not afford to make such a mistake. I warned the boarding team one last time. When my turn came I was relieved to have made it onto the ladder without incident. I had climbed Jacob's ladders before, but never one that was dangling in mid-air. If the rope ladder is not against the side of the ship your feet kick out at a forty-five-degree angle in front of you. As a result, approximately two-thirds of your body weight is on your arms. I needed 100 percent concentration. Let go with right hand, move it up above the next rung, grip tightly, let go with the left hand, move it up above the next rung, grip it tightly, lift right foot to the next rung, lift left foot to the next rung, repeat. I didn't care how long it took. I knew I could not afford to make any mistakes.

We all made it on board safely. The chief officer was waiting for us on deck. Prior to boarding, we had all hands, who were not on watch on the bridge or in the engine room, muster in the galley and that's where they were waiting for us. Crews on merchant ships are of many different nationalities. This ship had mostly Pakistani officers and Turkish crewmembers. Ship crews were always respectful toward the Coast Guard marine inspectors. However, they were not used to being boarded by armed Coast Guardsmen, and this time they were nervous. I sent half of the boarding team to search the ship and the rest I took to the galley to check the documents of all the crewmembers. The crew gathered in the galley was apparently anxious about what was going to happen. This was not normal, and it was their first entry into the U.S. following 9/11. I had the chief officer line them up and posted a boarding team member at the doorway. One by one I checked their passport and seafarer's identification document against the crew list that had been submitted in their notice of arrival. There were a number of name misspellings, so I radioed correct spellings back to the *Thetis* to run a check on the correct spellings.

"Sir, I think you need to come see this."

It was one of the boarding team members who had been searching the ship.

"I don't know if it means anything, but I think you should see it."

"OK, let's go."

He led me out into the dingy passageway with torn floor tiles.

"It's in here," he said stopping in front of a deck box against the wall.

He lifted the cover of the box where equipment is stored and pulled out a soiled front page of a foreign newspaper with a large picture of Osama Bin Laden on it.

"What is this, and why is it in the deck box?" I asked the Pakistani captain standing next to me.

"This is Turkish newspaper. I don't know what it says."

I could tell from the date it was from September 12.

"What's it doing in here?"

"I have no idea," the captain said, obviously annoyed that one of the crew had stashed something that could cause him problems.

I had no idea whether it was a legitimate newspaper kept as a souvenir, or a radical publication praising the great victory of Bin Laden and had been stashed upon our arrival.

"Captain, I need your Turkish crewmember who speaks the best English."

"Yes, of course, chief engineer."

He turned and yelled at a crewmember to get the chief engineer immediately. The chief engineer arrived in the passageway minutes later. He was very nervous and confused.

"Chief, tell me what this says."

I held up the newspaper in front of him. He looked at it for a second or two, then looked at me and said in broken English, "It say dis is real terrorist!"

If he was the best English speaking Turk on board, I knew I wasn't going to get much more information. He was either telling the truth, or telling me what he thought I wanted to hear. Either way, it didn't seem to be enough evidence to escalate the matter.

We let everyone go back to work and waited for the name check results to be radioed back to us. The weather was nice and we waited on deck with the captain for four hours. Everyone had calmed down and we had a good time talking with the captain about many things. He was highly educated and spoke freely about politics, religion, and radicals. Sailors have a bond that runs between them, no matter where they are from. They love going to sea, exploring new places, and enjoying their time ashore. The Pakistani captain's conversation inevitably devolved into good old sailor talk. He held out his hand in front of me with his fingers spread wide. His thumb was pointed straight up.

"Do you know what this is?"

"No."

"This is the life cycle of a man." He grabbed his thumb with his other hand. "This is a man in his teens." Then, he grabbed his index finger. "This is a man in his twenties." Next, he grabbed his middle finger, which was parallel to the deck. "This is a man in his thirties." He was smiling now in recognition of my awareness, and he grabbed his ring finger. "This is a man in his forties." Finally, he grabbed his pinky, pointing down at a forty-five-degree angle. "And this is a man in his fifties."

I nodded and smiled.

Then the captain said loudly, "I am in my fifties, but this is still me!" He grabbed his thumb and laughed hysterically.

After the results of the name checks came back, we released the ship and wished them a safe voyage. We climbed back down the Jacob's ladder and headed back to our own ship.

When we approached the next ship to board I made my way to the bridge of the *Thetis*. The officer started to call the ship on the radio. I walked past the captain over to the officer on watch and held out my hand.

"May I, sir?"

He looked at me, surprised, and then handed me the radio microphone. I directed the ship to come to all stop, rig the accommodation ladder, come about to make a lee, and stand by for a Coast Guard boarding. The ship agreed without hesitation.

"Thanks," I said as I handed the radio back to the officer on watch and headed below to get ready for the next boarding. Getting on board the ships was much safer after that.

For my involvement conducting those boardings as a Marine Safety Boarding Team Leader, I received the War on Terrorism Service Medal. It was as close to any war as I would get during my military career, and I was proud to have the opportunity to contribute to the cause.

When I got back home, I still felt like I wasn't doing enough, especially after watching people from New Orleans head to New York to feed gumbo to first responders. So, I made a sign reading:

Born and raised in Manhattan, all donations go to the victims' families in my hometown.

I went down to the French Quarter, opened my bagpipe case, stuck the sign in it and started playing. People gave generously. I made about forty-seven dollars per hour. I donated the money through the Ancient Order of Hibernians 9/11 fundraising efforts.

Although I didn't know him as an adult, Mike Armstrong was apparently as well-liked as he was as a kid. His friends in the restaurant and bar industry opened up an Irish pub in his honor at 19th Street and First Avenue in Manhattan, and named it M.J. Armstrong's. I went to visit the place during a benefit and paid my respects to his family. There is a plaque by the bar in his honor, and his name is etched in granite at the 9/11 Memorial. May his soul rest in peace.

CHAPTER 16

U.S. Coast Guard Pipe Band

In the summer of 2001, I became aware of the fact that in less than two years I would have two decades in the Coast Guard and could possibly retire. Although I wasn't ready to go, I knew that when the time came, if they tried to transfer me away from New Orleans I would have to retire instead of move. I had always heard of the Coast Guard Festival in Grand Haven, Michigan, but I had never given much thought to attending. I decided making a family trip to the Coast Guard Festival would be a great last hurrah.

Grand Haven was designated Coast Guard City U.S.A. by an Act of Congress signed by the President on November 13, 1998. The Coast Guard Festival dates back to an annual Coast Guard picnic, which started in 1924. The first festival was held in 1937 and has grown over the years to the ten-day festival we have today that is always scheduled to coincide with the Coast Guard's Birthday, August 4.[39]

I researched the festival, and I saw that it included a parade and a Coast Guard memorial service. Nothing screams bagpipes more than a parade and a memorial service. I started to think about how cool it would be if the Coast Guard had a bagpipe band to participate in the parade and memorial service. And that's when I decided to create one.

I always did things by the book. But now, as a chief warrant officer with 18 years in, I had gained the wisdom that if I followed strict military protocol, it would never happen. I knew that in all my time serving as a Coast Guard piper, I had never received even a hint of opposition. Trying to get official permission, however, was another thing altogether. I finally decided to embrace the boatswain's mate mantra that used to annoy me. "It's easier to be forgiven than it is to get permission."

I knew of a private, unofficial website used by Coast Guard people for Coast Guard stuff. The website was called Fred's Place, started by a retired radioman named Fred Siegel. I got on Fred's Place and posted that I was calling all Coast Guard bagpipers and drummers to form a pipe band for the 2002 Grand Haven Coast Guard Festival. I was amazed at the response. In no time, I had over twenty pipers and drummers wanting to participate and many more with words of encouragement.

On August 7, 2001, I sent a letter to Jerry Smith, the Executive Director of the Coast Guard Festival. I suggested the idea of having a Coast Guard bagpipe band participate in the parade and asked for his endorsement before I approached Coast Guard Headquarters. Jerry Smith ran the idea through the Festival Board of Directors and reported back that they would love to have us in the parade and were considering us for the memorial service as well.

I had decided I wasn't going to ask anyone's permission, so instead I decided I would simply tell everyone what we were doing and give them the opportunity to shut us down if they saw fit. Each of the five branches of the military has one person who holds the rank of E-10, the most senior enlisted person in each service. I decided to inform our E-10, the Master Chief Petty Officer of the Coast Guard Vince Patton, whose office was in Coast Guard Headquarters and who worked closely with the Commandant. I emailed the master chief on August 13, introduced myself, and told him what we were up to. I explained that the festival executive director thought it was a great idea and asked him what he thought of our idea and for any suggestions on actions we should take prior to moving forward.

Master Chief Patton emailed back on August 27. He said our idea sounded great and that it would be terrific to see such a fine group. He said it would add a touch of class if I could get it together.

I called the local Grand Haven Group Commander and told him what we intended to do. On August 28, he emailed back that the Ninth District Commander was receptive to our attendance and that I should do all coordinating through him. The only hint of concern that came from the master chief and the group commander was that we might need to deal with Headquarters if we were going to modify the uniform.

Through email, we voted on the uniform amongst all the pipers and drummers who expressed an interest in attending the event. We came up with a standardized Coast Guard bagpipe band uniform: tropical blue short-sleeved Coast Guard uniform shirt with all devices, black fore and aft cap called a glengarry with small blue feather known as a hackle, thick blue knee socks we call hose, white spats to cover our black military oxfords, black leather piper's belt, and a sporran of horse hair hanging down in front of the kilt. Everything would be uniform, with the exception of the kilts. We agreed to wear the kilts that we had. I called Bob Gitschier, the civilian employee in the Headquarters uniform branch that I had dealt with over the years, and gave him an update. His opinion regarding our uniform alteration was that as long as the district commander was in favor, we were good to go. On September 25, I emailed Master Chief Patton with an update. He responded that he thought it was great and that he had received an email from the Ninth Coast Guard District letting him know that they were "very excited about this idea." With that, it was all ahead full. I gave all levels of the chain of command the opportunity to put the kibosh on my idea, and instead, they all gave me the green light.

We continued to prepare throughout the year. We voted on a Drum Major, and we voted on a Pipe Major to be in charge of the music. We also voted on what tunes we would play. I made sure we had some Irish tunes along with the usual Scottish ones. The Pipe Major distributed standard tune settings for us all to practice. I was responsible for everything else.

About halfway through the year, I received a call from Commander Andrew Anderson, a retired Coast Guard commander and drum major for a local pipe band in Florida. Andy was excited about the idea and expressed his interest in joining us. I told him we would love to have him, but that we had already voted Michael Doria to be the drum major. Mike Doria was a third class petty officer who had been the drum major for the Citadel pipe band. Andy understood and said he would play the tenor drum for us.

Andy asked me if we were going to wear the Coast Guard tartan. I told him I had never heard of a Coast Guard tartan, so Andy filled me in. In 1997, Joanne Pendleton and her husband, Chief Warrant Officer Mike Pendleton, saw the West Point Pipe Band play. Mike Pendleton mentioned that it would be great if there was a Coast Guard tartan. Joanne was then inspired to make it happen and presented her husband with a Coast Guard tartan kilt for his retirement. In 1999, Joanne went to Commandant James Loy with her idea, which he strongly endorsed. The tartan design was based upon the Hamilton tartan, as Alexander Hamilton, the first Secretary of the Treasury, is considered to be the father of the Coast Guard. Andy Anderson was instrumental in getting the tartan approved by Admiral Loy on May 1, 2002.[40] While I was happy to hear of the Coast Guard tartan, I explained to Andy that given the short time frame and limited funds, we would have to forego the Coast Guard tartan kilts. All pipers and drummers were participating at their own expense and kilts cost $300-$400 each.

On the morning of Friday, August 2, 2002, on the grounds of Coast Guard Group Grand Haven, the U.S. Coast Guard Pipe Band gathered for the first time. Aware of the historical significance of this day, I made sure the first tune we played together was the official Coast Guard marching song, "Semper Paratus." Despite the fact that most of us had never met before, we sounded pretty darn good. The other members of the pipe band present at that initial event were: Andrew Anderson, Michael Doria, Michael Fink, Iain Anderson, Paul Rothwell, Steve Cochran, Michael Henry, Steve Young, Rene Blue O'Connell, and Jim Taylor.

That same afternoon we played "Amazing Grace" at the National Coast Guard Memorial Service in Escanaba Park along the banks of the Grand River. After the memorial service, we piped the Vice Commandant, Vice Admiral Ronald Barrett, into the American Legion Hall for the Enlisted Man's Dinner. We received great praise from everyone we encountered. The next day we led the Annual Coast Guard Festival Parade to cheering crowds. After the parade we played for our lunch at the annual Coast Guard Festival picnic. It was there that we had a conversation with Vice Admiral Barrett, the Vice Commandant of the Coast Guard. He said he really liked what we were doing and that he would like to see more of it. Andy Anderson was the only one of us wearing the Coast Guard tartan kilt. I had a solid green

Receiving a plaque, presented by the Commandant, ADM Thomas Collins, for founding the U.S. Coast Guard Pipe Band in 2002.

Irish kilt, which didn't look so good with a light blue uniform shirt. The Vice Commandant wanted to know why we all weren't wearing the Coast Guard tartan. He explained that the Coast Guard didn't have funds to support a pipe band, but that he would support our efforts as a voluntary, affiliated organization.

On September 6, 2002, Andy Anderson, our newly appointed Secretary and Treasurer, filed the paperwork and incorporated the U.S. Coast Guard Pipe Band. We became a private, non-profit entity that would be open to anyone who was legally authorized to wear the uniform: active duty, reserves, retirees,

Get REWARDED here, there, everywhere

Free checked bag[1] | Priority boarding

2 United Club℠ one-time passes

25% back on United® inflight purchases[2]

Earn miles on every purchase

Take off with the United℠ Explorer Card.

UnitedExplorerCard.com

REWARDED

UNITED Explorer MileagePlus
VISA Signature
D. BARRETT

[1]FREE CHECKED BAG: Free bag is for first standard checked bag for the primary Cardmember and one companion traveling on the same reservation. Purchase of ticket(s) with Card is required.

[2]Get 25% back as a statement credit on purchases of food, beverages and Wi-Fi onboard United-operated flights when you pay with your Explorer Card. Accounts subject to credit approval. Restrictions and limitations apply. United MileagePlus® credit cards are issued by Chase Bank USA, N.A. Offer subject to change. See UnitedExplorerCard.com for pricing and rewards details.

MileagePlus: Miles accrued, awards and benefits issued are subject to the rules of the United MileagePlus program. For details, see united.com.   CSM957

To comply with U.S. Department of Transportation and other country regulations, airlines are required to obtain the full name of customers traveling on international flights. Please complete the following. For applicability, please ask the United Representative.

(REQUIRED)

Last Name(s)/Surname(s)   Middle   First

(OPTIONAL)

Emergency Contact - Name/Relationship   Area Code of City &   Country Code & Phone

All information is confidential and by law cannot be used for commercial purposes.
See DRS reference: GG EME CTC

UNITED

TSA PRE

PRIORITY BOARD

SIMONDS/ANDREWBLAKE

TRAVERSE CITY TO CHICAGO

UA4527

THU SEPTEMBER 5 2019

TVC-ORD ✳✳✳✳ **6:20A**

GATE — BOARDING BEGINS:

BOARDING ENDS: 6:30 AM
FLIGHT DEPARTS: 6:45 AM
FLIGHT ARRIVES: 7:00 AM

WINDOW
ECONOMY

SEAT

15D

BOARDING GROUP

2

A STAR ALLIANCE MEMBER ✪

B9GXQV   15D
UA 4527   B5E1FD

48

auxiliarists, and honorably discharged wartime veterans. I was elected the first president, and everyone was outfitted in Coast Guard tartan kilts.

Steve Young, our Pipe Major and the guy who had taught me to play the pipes, piped at my retirement ceremony in March of 2003. I took an entire year to write my farewell address, which I delivered in about twenty minutes. I told the story of what the Coast Guard meant to me and only got choked up once when it came time to thank my wife for her love and support. I wanted to use the sword I had purchased upon being promoted to chief warrant officer at least once, and my commanding officer was kind enough to agree to "full dress blue with sword" as the official uniform. My four-year-old daughter Emma and I put the sword to good use by using it to cut the cake.

The Gilheany family at retirement: Stefanie, Emma, and me, March 2003.

I remembered feeling inspired the first time I saw a picture of a Coast Guard piper early in my career and decided to track him down. Mike Mone was a long-retired chief boatswain's mate living in New Hampshire. I was very happy when I finally got him on the phone and even happier when, after some arm-twisting, I got him to join the band.

The ranks of the band grew quickly with the help of many dedicated members. Allowing Coast Guard auxiliarists to be in the band was key, as it allowed many excellent pipers and drummers, not otherwise associated with the Coast Guard, to join the auxiliary in order to be in the band. We continued to perform at the Coast Guard Festival every year where we hold our annual general meeting. Coincidently, a historic event occurred early on in our existence as a band, which presented a great opportunity for us to serve and demonstrate the pipe band's value to the Coast Guard.

On June 6, 1968, Lieutenant Jack Rittichier's rescue helicopter was shot down in Laos while attempting to recover a downed Marine pilot. Lt. Rittichier's helicopter crashed in a ball of fire and he was officially designated "Killed in Action – Body not Recovered." He was the only missing Coast Guardsman from the Vietnam War. In February 2003, I heard that a Joint Task Force had located human remains possibly belonging to Lt. Rittichier in the jungles of Laos. The remains would be taken to the U.S. Army Central Identification Laboratory in Hawaii for identification. I assumed that if the remains were positively identified, they would be interred at Arlington Cemetery with full honors. This is one major reason we started the pipe band, and I felt strongly our services needed to be offered to the family through Coast Guard Headquarters. I called the lab in Hawaii and introduced myself and asked them to keep me apprised. As soon as the positive identification was made, I started working with Headquarters to have the pipe band included in the funeral services. On October 6, 2003, the remains of Lt. Rittichier arrived at Coast Guard Hill in Arlington National Cemetery on a caisson pulled by four white horses. There was a flyover by four helicopters, a twenty-one-gun salute and a bugler played taps. As the Commandant of the Coast Guard presented the flag to Lt. Rittichier's brother, the U.S. Coast Guard Pipe Band was playing "Amazing Grace."[41] It was a great honor to be included in this momentous event.

Word of the pipe band was spreading quickly. On August 15, 2006, the U.S. Coast Guard Pipe Band received written permission from Coast Guard Headquarters to use the Coast Guard's statutorily protected name in a letter signed by Rear Admiral Burhoe. Our involvement grew from individual pipers and drummers performing at funerals, changes of command, and retirement ceremonies to full band events. Soon we were receiving many requests, including an invitation the band proudly accepted, to play on stage with the Chieftains at the Kennedy Center in 2009. A Coast Guard Pipe Band piper even appeared in the movie *The Guardian* with Kevin Costner and Ashton Kutcher.

For me, however, there was no more important event than the New York City St. Patrick's Day Parade in 2008. One of our members, Mike Doria, had secured an invitation to the parade, the first invitation of a Coast Guard band to the parade. We had thirty-two pipers and drummers who had travelled from as far away as the Pacific Northwest, and we were the largest U.S. Armed Forces Pipe Band ever to perform in the history of the parade.[42]

Forming up for the St. Patrick's Day Parade in New York City, 2008.

It was another childhood dream coming true for me as I led the third column of the Coast Guard Pipe Band up Fifth Avenue. As we reached my neighborhood at the end of the route, I was very much aware of my blessings and how I once stood just over there on the sidewalk as a child, mesmerized by the sound of the pipes as they went by, dreaming a boyish dream.

Marching up Fifth Avenue on St. Patrick's Day 2008, heading for my old neighborhood.

Photo credit: Marla O'Neil

In 2011, at the Coast Guard Festival in Grand Haven, Michigan, Rear Admiral Parks presented me with the U.S. Coast Guard Public Service Commendation for having founded the U.S. Coast Guard Pipe Band:

> The Commandant of the Coast Guard takes great pleasure in presenting the United States Coast Guard Public Service Commendation to Chief Warrant Officer Kevin Gilheany, USCG (Ret.), founder of the U.S. Coast Guard Pipe Band. In 2001, CWO2 Kevin Gilheany called bagpipers and Highland drummers within the Coast Guard to meet at the Coast Guard Festival in Grand Haven, Michigan to honor the Coast Guard through fellowship and music. Ten years later, the Pipe Band has become a key part of the Grand Haven festival and its performances at the festival's memorial service and parade have become a cherished

summer tradition. Under his guidance and leadership, and with the approval of the Commandant, the Coast Guard Pipe Band was formed into a not-for-profit, private non-federal entity. CWO2 Gilheany was named as one of its founding directors and was the first president of the organization, serving in that capacity for nine years. Under his guidance and leadership the organization has grown to more than 100 members and has received more than 300 requests for performances at Coast Guard and community events. He has participated personally in more than 25 Pipe Band performances, supporting and bringing credit to the Coast Guard. He also serves as the Pipe Band's regional coordinator for the Eighth Coast Guard District, coordinating and planning requests for solo and detachment performances throughout the Gulf Coast and Midwest. Under CWO Gilheany's leadership, the Coast Guard Pipe Band has become the largest all-volunteer military Pipe Band in the United States. It promotes greater public understanding, recognition and appreciation of the history, traditions, contributions, sacrifices, roles and missions of the men and women of the U.S. Coast Guard. CWO Gilheany's support of the U.S. Coast Guard Pipe Band is most heartily commended and is in keeping with the highest traditions of the United States Coast Guard."[43]

On Friday, August 2, 2013, the City of Grand Haven, Michigan, Coast Guard City U.S.A., dedicated a plaque in their Walk of Coast Guard History, officially commemorating the Pipe Band's place in the history of the U.S. Coast Guard.

On Friday, June 1, 2018, upon request of the Commandant, ADM Paul F. Zukunft, members of the Pipe Band, dispatched by long-term Pipe Major M.L. Loudermilk, performed for the first time at the Commandant's Change of Command in Washington, D.C.

U.S. Coast Guard Pipe Band in the Seventh Regiment Armory, NYC, March 17, 2008. Author in fifth row up, right end.

Photo credit: Marla O'Neil

It occurred to me that I was not meant to be an enlisted Officer in Charge, a regular commissioned officer, or the skipper of a patrol boat. During my retirement ceremony my commanding officer, Captain Ronald Branch, had offered these remarks:

> Few people have the opportunity to leave a legacy on the Coast Guard. Mr. Gilheany, for the rest of your life when you see the Coast Guard pipers, you will know it was because of you. You have made a difference, and you should be very proud.

It was a great honor and blessing to be able to combine two of my passions in founding the U.S. Coast Guard Pipe Band and to have made a lasting impact in my own personal way.

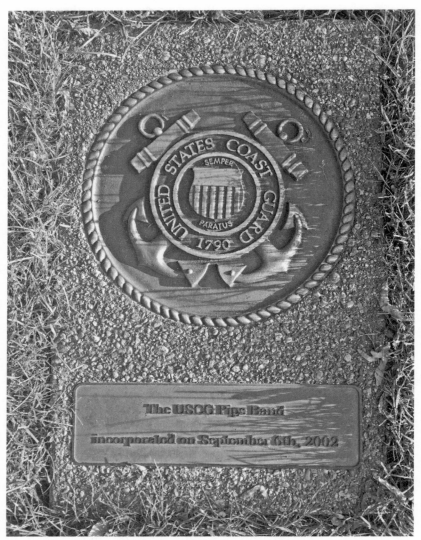

Plaque commemorating the founding of the USCG Pipe Band in the Walk of Coast Guard History, Grand Haven, Michigan.

My mother passed away in 2001. It would have been nice if she could have enjoyed the fruits of her efforts to inspire my dreams. As a young adult, I was often frustrated that my mother wouldn't do more for herself besides praying all the time. But, as a father, it occurred to me that maybe she wasn't trying to help herself. Maybe she was just praying for me.

In boot camp, I felt sorry for my fellow swim failure colleagues who were eventually sent home. But with age comes wisdom, and I now realize all things happen for a reason. Life is filled with constructive disappointments. It's how we react to them that determine whether we will become discouraged, or simply alter course. I hope my fellow recruits had faith and continued to pursue their dreams with vigor.

Endnotes

Chapter 2

1 Robert Erwin Johnson, *Guardians of the Sea* (Annapolis: United States Naval Institute, 1987), 1-2.

Chapter 4

2 "Carderock Division West Bethesda, MD," Global Security, accessed March 4, 2018, http://www.globalsecurity.org/military/facility/carderock.htm.

3 Commandant, U.S. Coast Guard, Coast Guard Meritorious Unit Commendation, awarded to U.S. Coast Guard 1985-86 Winter Law Enforcement Operation Forces, May 22, 1986.

4 Scott Packard, "How Guantanamo Bay Became the Place the U.S. Keeps Detainees," *The Atlantic*, September 4, 2013, https://www.theatlantic.com/national/archive/2013/09/how-guantanamo-bay-became-the-place-the-us-keeps-detainees/279308/.

5 "History of Santiago de Cuba," Santiago de Cuba, accessed March 4, 2018, http://www.santiago-de-cuba.net/history.htm.

6 "The World of 1898: The Spanish American War – Chronology," Library of Congress, accessed March 4, 2018, https://www.loc.gov/rr/hispanic/1898/chronology.html.

Chapter 5

7 "Average Weather in Norfolk," Weather Spark, accessed March 4, 2018, http://weatherspark.com/history/31160/1986/Norfolk-Virginia-United-States.

8 National Geographic, "Seconds from Disaster—Space Shuttle *Challenger*," released January 31, 2007, https://www.youtube.com/watch?v=rjSGIgb5f9w.

9 Douglas Martin, "Roger Boisjoly, 73, Dies; Warned of Shuttle Danger," *The New York Times*, February 3, 2012, http://www.nytimes.com/2012/02/04/us/roger-boisjoly-73-dies-warned-of-shuttle-danger.html.

10 National Geographic, "Seconds from Disaster."

11 National Geographic, "Seconds from Disaster."

12 "1986: Space Shuttle *Challenger* Disaster Live on CNN," Youtube, accessed March 4, 2018, https://www.youtube.com/watch?v=AfnvFnzs91s.

13 National Geographic, "Seconds from Disaster."

14 Commandant, Coast Guard Meritorious Unit Commendation.

15 William Harwood, "*Challenger* Wreckage May Be Stored in Silo," UPI, August 27, 1986, https://www.upi.com/Archives/1986/08/27/Challenger-wreckage -may-be-stored-in-silo/1196525499200/.

16 National Geographic, "Seconds from Disaster."

17 Committee on Science and Technology, House of Representatives, Ninety-Ninth Congress, Second Session, Report, "Investigation of the *Challenger* Accident," October 29, 1986, 4.

18 Committee on Science and Technology, "Investigation," 4.

19 Martin, "Roger Boisjoly."

20 NASA Administrator, NASA Certificate of Appreciation Space Shuttle *Challenger* Recovery Operations.

21 Committee on Science and Technology, "Investigation," 3.

Chapter 6

22 "Sikorsky HH52A "Seaguard"," United States Coast Guard Aviation History, accessed March 4, 2018, https://cgaviationhistory.org/aircraft_/ sikorsky-hh-52a-seaguard/.

Chapter 7

23 Gordon McGowan, *The Skipper and the Eagle* (Peekskill: Sea History Press, 1998), 17.

24 James Morgan, "Why is the US still using a Nazi tall ship?" *BBC News*, July 29, 2015, http://www.bbc.com/news/magazine-33543706.

25 McGowan, *The Skipper and the Eagle*, 8.

26 McGowan, *The Skipper and the Eagle*, 20-36.

27 McGowan, *The Skipper and the Eagle*, 90.

28 McGowan, *The Skipper and the Eagle*, 99.

29 McGowan, *The Skipper and the Eagle*, 229-30.

30 Tom Vesey, "Pride of Baltimore Captain Expressed Concern About Ship's Stability," *The Washington Post*, May 31, 1986, https://www.washingtonpost .com/archive/local/1986/05/31/pride-of-baltimore-captain-expressed -concern-about-ships-stability/899cedbc-33d1-4531-8d47-38bb9b923d1b /?utm_term=.cdd3cbfc9fe5.

31 "Engineering, Construction and Crossing the Atlantic," The Statue of Liberty-Ellis Island Foundation, Inc., accessed March 4, 2018. https://liberty ellisfoundation.org/statue-history.

32 "Weather History for New York, N.Y.," The Old Farmer's Almanac, accessed March 4, 2018, http://www.almanac.com/weather/history/NY/New+York.

Chapter 8

33 Robert Erwin Johnson, *Guardians of the Sea* (Annapolis: United States Naval Institute, 1987), 161-63.

Chapter 10

34 S. Frederick Starr, *Southern Comfort* (New York: Princeton Architectural Press, 1998), 42.

35 Starr, *Southern Comfort*, 71.

Chapter 11

36 Ralph Shanks, Wick York, Lisa Woo Shanks, *The U.S. Life-Saving Service* (Petaluma: Costano Books, 1996), 13.

37 Shanks, York, Shanks, *The U.S. Life-Saving Service*, 243.

Chapter 14

38 "History," *The Coast Guard Proceedings of the Marine Safety and Security Council*, Summer 2014, 9. http://uscgproceedings.epubxp.com/i/314313-sum-2014.

Chapter 16

39 "Festival History," Grand Haven Coast Guard Festival, accessed March 4, 2018, https://www.coastguardfest.org/about/.

40 "U.S. Coast Guard Tartan History," U.S. Coast Guard Pipe Band, accessed March 4, 2018, http://www.uscgpipeband.org/tartanhistory.php.

41 "Jack Columbus Rittichier," Arlington National Cemetery, accessed March 4, 2018, http://www.arlingtoncemetery.net/jcrittichier.htm.

42 Commandant, U.S. Coast Guard, Certificate of Merit, awarded to CWO Kevin P. Gilheany, USCG, Ret.

43 Commandant, U.S. Coast Guard, Coast Guard Public Service Commendation, awarded to CWO Kevin P. Gilheany, USCG, Ret.

Bibliography

Books

Johnson, Robert Erwin. *Guardians of the Sea*. Annapolis: United States Naval Institute, 1987.

McGowan, Gordon. *The Skipper and the Eagle*. Peekskill: Sea History Press, 1998.

Shanks, Ralph, Wick York, and Lisa Woo Shanks. *The U.S. Life-Saving Service*. Petaluma: Costano Books, 1996.

Starr, S. Frederick. *Southern Comfort*. New York: Princeton Architectural Press, 1998.

News or Magazine Articles

Harwood, William. "*Challenger* Wreckage May Be Stored in Silo." *UPI*, August 27, 1986, https://www.upi.com/Archives /1986/08/27/Challenger-wreckage-may-be-stored-in-silo/ 1196525499200/.

"History." *The Coast Guard Proceedings of the Marine Safety and Security Council*, Summer 2014, 9. http://uscgproceedings .epubxp.com/i/314313-sum-2014.

Martin, Douglas. "Roger Boisjoly, 73, Dies; Warned of Shuttle Danger." *The New York Times*, February 3, 2012, http://www .nytimes.com/2012/02/04/us/roger-boisjoly-73-dies-warned -of-shuttle-danger.html.

Morgan, James. "Why Is the US Still Using a Nazi Tall Ship?" *BBC News*, July 29, 2015, http://www.bbc.com/news/magazine -33543706.

Packard, Scott. "How Guantanamo Bay Became the Place the U.S. Keeps Detainees." *The Atlantic*, September 4, 2013, https://www.theatlantic.com/national/archive/2013/09/how -guantanamo-bay-became-the-place-the-us-keeps-detainees/ 279308/.

Vesey, Tom. "Pride of Baltimore Captain Expressed Concern About Ship's Stability." *The Washington Post*, May 31, 1986 https://www.washingtonpost.com/archive/local/1986/05/31 /pride-of-baltimore-captain-expressed-concern-about-ships -stability/899cedbc-33d1-4531-8d47-38bb9b923d1b/?utm _term=.cdd3cbfc9fe5.

Government Reports

Committee on Science and Technology, House of Representatives, Ninety-Ninth Congress, Second Session. Report. "Investigation of the *Challenger* Accident." October 29, 1986.

Website Content

Arlington National Cemetery, "Jack Columbus Rittichier," Accessed March 4, 2018, http://www.arlingtoncemetery.net /jcrittichier.htm.

Global Security. "Carderock Division West Bethesda, MD." Accessed March 4, 2018. http://www.globalsecurity.org/mili tary/facility/carderock.htm.

Grand Haven Coast Guard Festival. "Festival History." Accessed March 4, 2018. https://www.coastguardfest.org/about/.

Library of Congress. "The World of 1898: The Spanish American War—Chronology." Accessed March 4, 2018. https://www.loc .gov/rr/hispanic/1898/chronology.html.

National Geographic. "Seconds from Disaster—Space Shuttle *Challenger*," released January 31, 2007. https://www.youtube .com/watch?v=rjSGIgb5f9w.

Santiago de Cuba. "History of Santiago de Cuba." Accessed March 4, 2018. http://www.santiago-de-cuba.net/history.htm.

The Old Farmer's Almanac. "Weather History for New York, N.Y." Accessed March 4, 2018. http://www.almanac.com/weather /history/NY/New+York.

The Statue of Liberty-Ellis Island Foundation, Inc. "Engineering, Construction and Crossing the Atlantic." Accessed March 4, 2018. https://libertyellisfoundation.org/statue-history.

United States Coast Guard Aviation History. "Sikorsky HH52A "Seaguard"." Accessed March 4, 2018. https://cgaviationhistory .org/aircraft_/sikorsky-hh-52a-seaguard/.

U.S. Coast Guard Pipe Band. "U.S. Coast Guard Tartan History." Accessed March 4, 2018, http://www.uscgpipeband.org/tartan history.php.

Weather Spark. "Average Weather in Norfolk." Accessed March 4, 2018. http://weatherspark.com/history/31160/1986/Norfolk -Virginia-United-States.

Youtube. "1986: Space Shuttle *Challenger* Disaster Live on CNN," Accessed March 4, 2018. https://www.youtube.com/watch?v =AfnvFnzs91s.

Award Citations

Commandant, U.S Coast Guard, Coast Guard Meritorious Unit Commendation, awarded to U.S. Coast Guard 1985-86 Winter Law Enforcement Operation Forces, May 22, 1986.

Commandant, U.S. Coast Guard, Certificate of Merit, awarded to CWO Kevin P. Gilheany, USCG, Ret.

Commandant, U.S. Coast Guard, Coast Guard Public Service Commendation, awarded to CWO Kevin P. Gilheany, USCG, Ret.

NASA Administrator, NASA Certificate of Appreciation Space Shuttle *Challenger* Recovery Operations.

Index